THRIVE!

STOP WISHING YOUR LIFE AWAY

ALAN WEISS

Other Works by Alan Weiss

Books

Best Laid Plans
Getting Started in Consulting (3rd ed.) (also in Chinese)
Good Enough Isn't Enough (also in Spanish)
Great Consulting Challenges
How to Acquire Clients
How to Establish A Unique Brand in the Consulting Profession
How to Market, Brand, and Sell Professional Services
How to Sell New Business and Expand Existing Business
How to Write A Proposal That's Accepted Every Time (2nd ed.)
Life Balance
Managing for Peak Performance (also in German)
Million Dollar Consulting (4th ed.) (also in Korean, Chinese, and Russian)
Money Talks (also in Chinese)
Organizational Consulting
Our Emperors Have No Clothes
Process Consulting
The Global Consultant (with Omar Kahn)
The Great Big Book of Process Visuals
The Innovation Formula (with Mike Robert) (also in German and Italian)
The Power of Strategic Commitment (with Josh Leibner and Gerson Mader)
The Second Great Big Book of Process Visuals
The Talent Advantage (with Nancy MacKay)
The Ultimate Consultant
The Unofficial Guide to Power Management
Value Based Fees (2nd ed.)

Booklets

Doing Well By Doing Right
How to Maximize Fees
Leadership Every Day
Raising the Bar
Rejoicing in Diversity

Newsletter

Balancing Act: Blending Life, Work, and Relationships®

THRIVE!

STOP WISHING YOUR LIFE AWAY

ALAN WEISS

Las Brisas Research Press
Summit Consulting Group, Inc.
Box 1009
East Greenwich, RI 02818
(800) 766-7935 • (401) 884-2778

Dedication

To my mother and father,
Jack and Roseanna Weiss, 94 and 88, respectively,
and my twin granddaughters,
Alaina Marie and Gabrielle Victoria, 1.

May that span of time demonstrate
the continuity and constancy of life, love and family.

Acknowledgments

My gratitude to Dr. Terry Giblin and Dr. Bob Cohen,
therapists extraordinaire. Terry taught me that it's about success,
not perfection; and Bob taught me to appreciate
the full colors of the palette of success.

My thanks to Chad Barr, technology genius,
who has provided me with websites, blogs, forums, and magic
to build and enhance my learning communities.

In memory of Ben Tregoe, the closest to a genius
that I've ever stood, co-founder of Kepner-Tregoe in Princeton,
who helped show me the world by pushing me into it.

For Koufax, the white German Shepherd, and Buddy Beagle,
loyal companions and fellow gourmands.
May we always race with our heads out the window.

And mostly for the lovely Maria,
who can still laugh at my humor, put up with my idiosyncrasies,
and successfully navigate the boat after 41 years.
Full speed ahead.

THRIVE!

Las Brisas Research Press
Summit Consulting Group, Inc.
Box 1009
East Greenwich, RI 02818

For general information about Alan Weiss's products, speaking, and consulting services please call (800) 766-7935 or (401) 884-2778. Our fax number is (401) 884-5068, and our email is info@summitconsulting.com. There are hundreds of free, indexed articles to download at www.summitconsulting.com. You may also subscribe at that site to our free, electronic newsletter *Balancing Act: Blending Life, Work, and Relationships*® and *Alan Weiss's Monday Morning Memo.*^{SM} Visit our blog with text, audio, and video postings daily at www.contarianconsulting.com

ISBN: 978-1-928611-15-8
Manufactured in the United States of America.
First edition.

Table of contents

Chapter 1!

When you wish upon a star....

- Children are instructed to make wishes
  so that parents don't have to pay attention, *19*
- People wish because they think they have no alternatives, *22*
- People wish because they are afraid to take action, *26*
- People wish because they are lazy, *28*
- People wish because they have become professional victims, *32*
- Summary: non-wishful thinking, *35*

Chapter one sets the stage by discussing the motivation for wishing as opposed to action, and why it's become an unconscious default position.

Chapter 2!

Wishing is to achievement what watching TV is to aerobic fitness

- Why do those lottery lines only begin to appear at the $100 million mark?, *37*
- Lord Acton got it wrong about power and corruption, *42*
- My favorite country song title is, "If I had shot her when I
  wanted to, I would have been out by now," *47*
- If you want to lose weight, stop eating so much, *52*

Chapter two examines personal accountability and how less energy in action outperforms more energy invested in wishing.

Chapter 9!

The five traits of the masters of their fates

- Trait 1—Resilience: The lessons of the ice plant, *172*
- Trait 2—Eternal learning: "It's not a problem" IS a problem, *174*
- Trait 3—Self-esteem: "Follow me!", *177*
- Trait 4—Perseverance: You win some, you lose some, and some get rained out, but you have to suit up for them all, *182*
- Trait 5—Love: No one says, "For the 'like' of God….," *184*

Chapter nine provides the five primary factors the author has discovered to create mastery and not wishful thinking.

Chapter 10!

TIAABB: There is always a bigger boat

- Wealth is more about discretionary time than money, *189*
- Happiness is synthetic, not organic, *193*
- Success always trumps perfection, *196*
- Happiness is *not* just a thing called "dough," *201*
- The Runner, *205*

Chapter ten proves that life is not about the best, the most, or the biggest, but about personal, customized happiness, which is self-created.

Chapter 11!

Making your dreams come true

- Move three things forward a mile, not a hundred things forward an inch, *209*
- The power of Tools for Change: The 1% Solution®, *213*
- Avoid the feedback pinball machine, *217*
- Stop crying, get up, and hit someone, *221*
- Making it so, *225*

Chapter eleven summarizes the steps one must take to create a Thriving life and, as Captain Picard would order on the Starship Enterprise, "Make it so."

Appendix

Introduction

We've all heard the moans and groans: "I wish I had said something at the time," or "I wish I had taken the risk of that new job," or "I wish I had bought the property when I could have...."

People are wishing their lives away. Coupled with the bizarre growth of victimhood mentalities over the last two decades, we are doing less and blaming more. We wished we had done something, but someone or some circumstance or some event stopped us. Or, so we'd like to believe.

I've found that organizations rarely have unhappy employees and happy customers. Similarly, poor relationship and an unhappy life seldom produce prosperous professions and business success. *We often confuse the dedication to work as the cause of broken relationships. The cracks and stress points were there to begin with, don't blame the job.*

My work as a coach, counselor, and global management consultant for the past 25 years, has provided overwhelming evidence of the connection between personal fulfillment and business success, but with a different etiology than most suspect. Too many of us don't take action, tend to stew and vacillate, and otherwise procrastinate, and then blame the weather, the fates, the government, or Bill Gates when we realize we've missed our window of opportunity.

Life is about success, not perfection. Waiting for the "perfect moment" is merely an excuse not to act. If perfection were the key, few planes would ever leave the ground, we would never have invented penicillin, and no one would ever attempt to play golf (or at least use a one iron). The fact that we have become adept at commiserating with each other about what "they" are doing to us, and believe that the problem is with "them," simply exacerbates the dilemma.

Thrive! is about doing much more than merely surviving, which is what most victims try to do. It is about personal mastery and business superiority through the identification of those techniques and approaches which you can use, pragmatically, every single day. There are no planners or six-month regimens here, largely because I'm into immediate gratification. On every page, you'll learn something you can use immediately. Now. Not in the morning. Now.

One more thing: This is not one of those self-help books where the only person really helped is the author. As George Carlin pointed out, "If it's someone else's book, it's not *self*-help!" I've distilled over a quarter of a century of learning, patterns, and trial and error within these 200+ pages. My intent is to help you help yourself. It's my advice and your discipline. We can't do it the other way around.

You may be helping me by buying this book, but your return on investment is going to be a thousand-fold. If you improve by 1% a day, in 70 days you'll be twice as good. That's my Tools for Change: The 1% Solution® and the wonder of compound *personal* interest. If you're not motivated by that, then this introduction has saved you the reading of the 200 pages and only cost you a few bucks.

But if you are interested, you've spent a pittance to embark on a great personal and career journey. Are you ready?

—Alan Weiss
East Greenwich, RI

Preface

One day when I was five years old I sat on a dirty stair in a cold, institutional hallway awaiting my father, who had disappeared through a foreboding looking door at the top of the staircase, far above me. I couldn't understand why I was being left in this dank, foreign place, an act which today would no doubt bring charges of child abandonment at least and abuse at most. His words of comfort to me were, "Don't move."

I found out years later that my father had gone to plead his case in a loan office. He had poor credit, a bank wouldn't touch us, and he had to bargain with the kinds of guys who would call us late in the evening and make threats when a $20 payment was late. He either didn't want me to experience the discussion or assumed I would be a hindrance, since I tended to cry at air-raid decibel levels when a button on my shirt came undone. (Yes, we had air-raid sirens and drills "back then.") You can imagine what might have occurred had I thought we would lose our four-room apartment.

It was an early exposure to a David Mamet play, before there was a David Mamet. "Glengarry Glen Rent," if you will.

I wasn't sure what was in store for me because most people around us were poor in the early 1950s. Some people still had phones with party lines and ice boxes instead of refrigerators. But I can tell you this: I never dreamed I'd ever stand in front of large audiences to inform and entertain them; I didn't think it possible that I could write a book; I assumed that wealthier, better educated individuals would call the shots should I happened to be in the same room. Never did I think it conceivable that the CEO of a Fortune 25 firm would turn to me for advice, or that I'd be making as much or more money than my client.

Columbia University turned me down, as it should have, since no one prepared me for the interview, during which I gave a superb performance of a mime stunned by an approaching locomotive's air horn. Rutgers, thank the gods, accepted me in a stroke of good fortune that I can't overemphasize. I had only applied to two schools, such was my lack of mentoring, lack of practicality, and lack of anything percolating in my cerebral cortex. Fortunately, Rutgers was and is one of the great public schools extant (and even learning how to play football pretty well).

But I've learned that a successful life involves just such a handful of landmark events. I was an exchange student during the summer between my junior and senior years in high school. (My counterpart from Finland, Esko, is currently the Finnish Ambassador to Paris. I consistently beat him at poker traveling through Europe. One hopes he plays better today, in diplomatic circles.) I narrowly and accidentally avoided the Viet Nam War draft, but I was drafted out of Prudential Insurance by a training firm in Princeton that provided my first mentor, Ben Tregoe, and my ticket to consulting. And, not incidentally, I married my high school sweetheart, Maria, along the way. It was much too early, much too naïve, and it has been much too good to believe. (She tells career women today, who ask how she can be comfortable "not working," that she did her work 40 years ago when she married a frog and made him into a prince, and is now living off the dividends.)

I realize that none of you reading this can play poker with Esko, go back to marry your high school sweetheart, or perhaps even find a firm that shows you the world. Frankly, I hate the "show and tell" books from executives who believe that readers can simply emulate what they have done. Their paths are interesting, but they usually are off-limits to others.

My intent here is different. I've distilled the processes, attitudes, beliefs, behaviors, and pure chutzpah that have accounted for my personal happiness, which has led to my business and professional success. I've enabled thousands of people I've coached and mentored to use these approaches successfully all over the globe, *so I have validated that they are transferable and they work.* There are more successful, better known people than I, but I have come farther than most and lead an incredible life that you, too, can lead if you choose, because success is all about choices.

Wishing gains you nothing, but decisions can change everything.

I don't suggest you be anything other than who you are, but I do advocate that you be all that you are. There is no arbitrary bar to leap or finish line to cross, but there is the challenge of realizing your own potential. Not many people I've met meet that challenge. Some have a poor attitude and some lack skills. Within these pages, you'll have the opportunity to overcome both deficits, if necessary.

I never received the valuable advice that a Donald Trump acquired from his father ("Here's a fortune, don't lose it!"). But my father, alive at this writing at 94, managed to convince enough people to lend him enough money to pay enough bills, so that I had food, clothing, and shelter, however tenuous at times.

There are legacies and there are legacies. I hope to add to mine with this book. You don't owe me a thing beyond the purchase price, although I believe you'll be surpassing your own expectations if you follow my advice. Don't worry about risk, whatever you do. As you read this, you're sitting on a rock hurtling at 85,000 miles per hour around a constantly exploding star. Do you get my drift?

However, the next time you see a kid sitting miserably by himself on a stairway, put your hand on his or her shoulder and whisper quietly, "Don't worry, it's going to be all right."

"Hell, it's going to be the ride of your life!"

THRIVE!

CHAPTER 1

When you wish upon a star....
You're probably psychotic

A lbert Einstein, that ultimate rationalist of the cosmos, often spoke of "the old one," which I infer to mean a God who set the clockwork in motion that Einstein was trying to analyze and explain. He also noted on several occasions that "God doesn't play dice."

The ability to Thrive is in direct correlation to the ability to stop kidding yourself. There is no old guy sitting amidst the heavens with a green eye shade and sleeve protectors in a tonitruous lather trying to mete out liberty and justice for all. I don't care if you believe in evolution or intelligent design.

But if you intend to accomplish important goals tomorrow by wishing things would change for you, you're going to have a long and unhappy life.

Children are instructed to make wishes so that parents don't have to pay attention

We are inculcated from zygoteness to wish for things. This early, learned behavior insinuates itself into our cerebral cortex like crabgrass in a lawn. Children are admonished to hope for things rather than provided with skills to deal with likely events. Disney admonished us all that "When you wish upon a star...." anything can happen. Of course, I believe that was a cricket holding forth.

This attitude stands us in poor stead. Wishing that the local bully doesn't visit the schoolyard that afternoon is a poor substitute for learning ways to rally the other kids against him; talking him out of his animosity; or mastering skills to beat the hell out of him. I remember how I wished that I had the ability to crush the very life force out of Richie Thompson, or that one of the high school linebackers would happen along when Thompson was using me for kickball practice.

But no one had taught me at that point to organize, influence, or throw a right cross, so Thompson continued to beat the crap out of me and everybody else.

We have serious emotional and growth needs that go unattended when we are young. You may well be denying your own kids and others the help they need right now. That's because:

- **The family dinner table has disappeared**. The traditional assembly point for grievances, learning, debate, and trial-and-error has been eradicated by extracurricular activities; two-income parents; technological diversion; cable television; texting; and the siren-like lure of being able to ship kids to a mall, neighbor's, ex-spouse's, or community banality.

- **We buy kids off with loot**. We give them cell phones, video games, fancy bikes, computers, and extraordinary privacy so that they won't intrude on our own precious discretionary time. Those kids who made pipe bombs and stockpiled munitions to cause the carnage at Columbine High School did so *in their rooms under their parents' roofs*. Underage girls arrange to meet predators on the Internet, on their personal computers, in the privacy of their own rooms.

- **Religious institutions have sacrificed their credibility**. Although Catholicism in the United States, for example, has increased by about 40 million people over the past 25 years, the number of priests (and therefore parishes and schools that can be supported) has dropped precipitously. The sexual abuse by some members of the clergy, though perpetrated by a tiny percentage of priests, was covered up and hidden by a significant number of bishops. Evangelicals and Fundamentalists have watched scandal after scandal taint highly visible leaders. Muslims have had their faith distorted by murderous thugs preaching a distorted version of jihad. Mainstream Protestants are facing schism over the role of gays in the clergy and as married members of the laity.[1] From Jimmy Swaggart to Jesse Jackson, the moral high ground has been eroded by immoral behavior and unethical conduct.

- **The business community has lost its moral compass.** Aside from the egregious cases of Enron, Adelphia, Tyco, Bernie Madoff, and the rest, we're seeing obscene multiples of pay for CEOs contrasted with front-line workers—in fact, the highest in the world, by far. Recalls affect everything from meat[2] to children's toys. The admonition of George Merck, founder of the pharmaceutical company which, long ago, was voted "Most Admired Company in America" in Fortune Magazine's annual poll for five years running, was "Do good and good will follow." He meant that an organization contributing to the environment would reap profits. What has occurred is that profits trump all else.

- **The schools are a quagmire of politics, unions, political correctness, and tribalism.** Even the best teachers are under pressure to adhere to standardized testing metrics, leave no child not only "behind" but with a substandard grade, and bring organization to a classroom where parents aren't involved and students with severe learning and physical disabilities are "mainstreamed."

---

[1] These are global phenomena. As I write this, a bishop in Tanzania has been forced to resign because of marital infidelity.

[2] At this writing, the 60-year-old Topps Meat Company had to close shop because of a meat recall that represented the equivalent of its entire year's production—millions of pounds of E. coli-tainted beef.

Unfortunately, teachers are rewarded for living long, not for classroom achievement, since tenure and ensuring "step increases" are simply based on showing up day after day. (Teachers score the lowest on SATs, GREs, and advanced placement tests of all professions. The best and the brightest are not going into teaching anymore.)

Kids, consequently, are being cheated by a society that is buying them off instead of bringing them up. The fantasy world in which they indulge (on the Internet, within television shows, during video games, even in text messaging) becomes their predominant world. *Wishing takes the place of achieving.* And as they grow into adolescence and adulthood, they emerge as us: accustomed to wishing for better times, accompanied by the conviction that we have no power to direct our lives or master our fates.

People wish because they think they have no alternatives

Social security is bankrupt; you can't do anything about the weather; it's impossible for a ....(white male, black female, gay man, opinionated woman, observant Jew, Ugandan with an accent, person over 50, person under 50, yada yada yada).... to advance in this organization; our neighbors are slobs and are ruining our property values; the Red Sox are cursed; the quiz shows are fixed.

"Most men lead lives of quiet desperation" seems positively uplifting after I talk to a great many people. They'd have to be personally motivated by Tony Robbins dragging them across volcanic ashes just to rise to the level of desperation. Theodore Dreiser observed—about 75 years ago—that "life is a dirty, stinking, treacherous game, and 99 men out of a hundred are bastards."

Not exactly a thought that propels you out of bed in the morning and that was quite a few wars ago and well before nuclear proliferation, the threat of global warming, new epidemics, and the advent of Paris Hilton.

An overly complex world has paralyzed us. It was far easier to buy a car when there were 16 choices from 5 manufacturers. You bought an Olds 88 or a Ford Fairlane. Today, there are thousands of permutations, and people have to resort to reference materials to try to figure out what makes sense[3] (and even who's still in business and owned by what other company).

Try to choose a high definition television. What size screen do you want? Would you like plasma, LCD, PCV, or LSD? Surround sound or SAP or stereo? How about cable, or fiber optic, or satellite, or a combination thereof? Would you like DVD, VHS, or DDS capability? Do you want Apple TV, Slingbox, and a universal remote to replace the nine separate ones? The choices are plethoric.

The more choices people have, the *lower* the ability to achieve happiness and the longer people take to make those choices, sometimes procrastinating into abject inaction. Even in the best of times, many people leave their retirement money in low-paying money fund accounts because it is too painful to try to choose among the myriad of investment options, even though they offer better returns.

I've received DVD instruction videos for my balcony awning, my car's entertainment system, and my pool robot. I can receive 260 satellite radio stations, but I've programmed only six and listen to just four of those with regularity. Our cable system has 900+ choices, but our television viewing is confined to about 12 channels.

We are lost in a world of choice which, paradoxically, robs us of the ability to make comfortable and rapid choices. So we don't choose from among the time-share alternative vacation spots, and we refrain from selecting a new computer, and we vacillate about refurnishing the family room.

---

[3] The Bentley GTC I drive is arguably the only one of its kind in the world. I chose the various woods, leathers, paint, carpets, and so on using a computer program called a "configurator." The permutations ran into the millions. It was actually tedious after a while, not a feeling you are supposed to have with a Bentley.

Because, *what if we make a choice that isn't optimal?* We are intrinsically afraid that we will select an alternative that isn't perfect, and although the Caymans are wonderful, it turns out that the hotel was more luxurious on Nevis; even though we love the new family room carpet on sale, we've learned that Pirgo® would have provided a more durable flooring; and while the Mac is a great looking new computer with an interface into the meaning of existence itself, we're led to believe that there will be a meaning of existence version 3.4.2 coming out in the not too distant future.

And so you will hear me harp on the following again and again:

Life is about success, not perfection.

That is a tough proposition for people to embrace. The thought that the 14,000 varieties of fish surrounding Grand Cayman are actually surpassed by the 16,500 critters hanging around Nevis is enough to make you just stay home and watch the Discovery Channel (or *Shark Attack*).

Irony of ironies, a world of increasing options has actually heightened our belief that we have no control and thwarts us from taking action. Instead, we wish that we could find the perfect spot/partner/drink/plumber/car/ring-tone. Of course, we can't. That's because there is no such thing as perfection, only success. But it takes a highly confident person to be satisfied with mere success!

I have friends who are constantly upgrading everything upgradeable in their lives: computers, cameras, big screen TVs, microwaves, fantasy football leagues, spouses. They are continually searching for something they will never find. If we applied this irrational quest to our entire lives without fear of the law or social retribution, none of us would stay married for, oh, I don't know—three weeks?!

We set ourselves up for an impotence that no blue pill can combat.[4] But there are environmental supports for learned helplessness:

- **We don't vote, so we get the government we deserve**. Less than half the U.S. population turns out for most elections, one of the lowest rates in the industrialized world, even post-Obama.

- **We don't read or analyze.** So we get our information from media sound bites, which are to understanding what reality television is to performing art. Twitter allows only 140 characters for communications, and most users don't need them all!

- **We no longer talk or personally communicate**. The art of letter writing is dead. The salon of the great hostess is extinct. We resort to text messages, hurried cell calls, and tangential conversation during other activities, such as golf, movies, and pub crawling. Facebook is a banal attempt to overcome Naisbitt's original (and accurate) "high tech/high touch"[5] relationship by using high tech to create high touch. Unless you care about whether someone has showered tonight or not, it doesn't work very well.

We tend to wish because we've set ourselves up in lives which seem to be largely out of our control, whether ceded, conceded, or receded.

---

[4] Even here, we're faced with being ready in an hour, or for 36 hours, or when stimulated, or when we hear a duck quack. The choices are ridiculous and emasculating in and of themselves. And I doubt that most men believe that it's a physician they should see first "if the erection lasts for more than four hours."

[5] *Megatrends,* by John Naisbitt (Warner Books, 1988).

People wish because they are afraid to take action

Even when choices are clear, or perfection seems like an attainable goal, we hesitate.

"I wish she would stop nitpicking my approaches at the strategy meetings. We're supposed to be at 50,000 feet, not ground level. She throws me off-stride with her narrow vision."

"Why don't you point that out at the time?"

"Oh, I could never do that. I'd be seen as defensive or not a team player."

"Why don't you talk to her privately after the meeting and explain your reactions?"

"She'd see that as a sign of weakness on my part, and would probably tell everyone."

"Why don't you tell the task force chair that her responses are dysfunctional?"

"Right, and be seen as asking someone else to protect me?"

"Then why don't you just learn to cope with it and stop whining?!"

"I just wish there was something I could do...."

We hear these specious arguments all the time. No course of actual action is agreeable so we just have to wish that something will change: She'll see the error of her ways; the boss will step in; someone else will quiet her; she'll be hit by a huge safe that Wile E. Coyote had purchased from the Acme Co. and was actually aiming at the Road Runner. (Beep! Beep!)

Think about how often all of us refuse the option of action and abuse the nonsense of wishing:

- "I wish this stupid cold would disappear." (Get some medication. Go to the doctor. Visit the pharmacist. Don't go to the meeting. Pass up your workout. Drink chicken soup.)

- "I wish we could, just once, have a happy holiday family gathering." (Don't play one-upsmanship with your cousin. Stock the Scotch your father-in-law always asks for. Stop engaging in gossip about your niece and her weight. Permit others to choose the music. Allow the football game to be on the TV.)

- "I wish I could lose this weight." (Go to the gym and get a personal trainer. Have a nutritionist create a diet. Stop snacking. Don't create an unreasonable expectation for your age and lifestyle. Walk up the stairs instead of taking the elevator. Park farther from the building.)

- "I wish I could close business better." (Learn closing skills from a coach or mentor. Read some books on sales. Practice on low-threat opportunities. Study the client's needs before you open your mouth. Use language that stresses value and not price.)

- "I wish we had a lawn like the neighbors." (Hire a lawn care outfit. Learn about nitrogen, acidity, fertilizers, and manure. Buy a better mower. Ask your neighbor for advice. Install in-ground sprinklers.)

This amount of aberrant wishing is occurring daily, to the extent that even Jiminy Cricket would shout, "Enough! Give the star a rest! I was lying. Your dreams *don't* come true. It's just a *song*, for God's sake!" (And you've become co-dependent on a talking cricket.)

We fear taking action for a few reasons, but the primary one is a fear of failure. I've noticed that the greatest cause of lack of success among the entrepreneurs and executives I've coached is low self-esteem. And low self-esteem drives people away from risk, rejection, and reality.

I've been able to stand toe-to-toe with tough executive clients because I've been thrown out of better rooms than that one and probably will be again. But, as Yvonne de Carlo sings in the fabulous Follies, "I'm Still Here." Failure is seldom fatal for the vast majority of us.

Every day, police officers all over the country strap on guns and go to work. And while an officer in New York City will probably serve until his or her retirement without drawing that gun in the line of duty, there will be cops in Peoria or Des Moines or Austin who will draw it and who will be killed. Every day, you put your life on the line in police work.

Our lives are not so treacherous, and the chances are rather good that we're not going to be shot in our lines of work, no matter how much someone else is saying, "I wish I had a gun and it was legal to kill accountants!" Fortunately, some wishing has salutary effects.

We can't fear failure. If you're not failing, you're just not trying. The penalty for failure isn't death, but the penalty for fearing to fail is mediocrity and the resort to wishing that, well, it were open season on accountants.

People wish because they are lazy

We have become sloth-like in our approach to our lives and work. Because of distractions and perceived complexity, we find it easier to wish than to do. We watch, but don't act. There is a certain lubricity in our voyeurism of those who do act.

In Rhode Island, where I live, half the drivers don't use turn signals, which are rather important on interstates where people are cruising at 80 mph. If you intend to enter the lane ahead of me, I'd just love to know. If you want me to stay off your tail as you make a turn into a driveway, just give me a sign. On most modern cars, a small flick of the signal indicator *automatically* provides three directional flashes. It takes an ounce of energy and a tenth of a second of thought.

But half don't bother. I doubt it's a religious or cultural observance, or the belief that their souls will be somehow stolen if they use a turn signal. It's simply pure laziness.

"I wish I could get someone to fix that porch" is somehow insufficient compared to "I'm going to take 30 minutes to find a carpenter." Telling your child from the couch, "I wish you'd stop picking on your sister" is not quite as effective as strolling over there, pulling them apart, and threatening your son with bodily harm (or at least hitting him upside the head with a Dr. Spock book).

We had Frank Sinatra come to Providence on one of his many farewell tours and I realized that this might be my last chance to see an American icon. I got on the horn, contacted several ticket brokers, and scored some wonderful seats. Friends were impressed and regretted not seeing him (or seeing him from such a distance he looked like a performing flea). I told them of the work and forethought I had put into this once the tour was announced.

"Gee," one said speaking for many, "I wish I had done that."

People wish for things that they didn't acquire or feel they cannot obtain. We are all wallowing in this kaleidoscope of inactivity at times. Here's why:

The police siren effect of time

We believe we have more time than we actually do, and consequently delay our actions until too late. Modern police and emergency sirens feature a peculiar Doppler Effect: You can't tell the direction from which they emanate, and by the time you do, the vehicle is almost in your lap. An experiment with equivalent sound conducted on gerbils would draw the wrath of the ASPCA, but there it is.

Similarly, we know that a deadline is looming or an event approaching, but we miscalculate the "buffer zone" between us and missing the boat. If you don't believe that, I suggest you contemplate the following nutso phenomena:

- People habitually shopping for Christmas presents on December 24th, when the pressure is unbearable, the crowds surly, and the good stuff already long gone.

- Frenetic payment of income taxes at midnight on April 14, with the postal service staying open late and providing huge bins in the middle of the street, creating a drive-by tax remittance system. Do you really think you've done the best job with your numbers in that circus?

- Forgive the gender-specific reference, but how many guys wait until the very morning of their wife's or girlfriend's birthday to even consider buying the card, much less the present? These even include the guys who are using turn signals.

The triumph of bureaucracy over the little person

I have to admit that I'm prone to simply tell my travel agent to buy a first class ticket rather than to do battle with the dark world of frequent flyer points. Transferring Amex to Continental, and using Sheraton to convert to USAir in order to use on United—well, it's daunting. And it takes 45 minutes of phone time (41.3 minutes on hold hearing that the call may be recorded for my protection and being advised that I should press "1" if I want to converse in English) only to find out that the blackout periods are chosen by pigeons pecking at red rectangles and blue diamonds for food pellets the night prior.

It's easier to spend $2,500 on a first class ticket than it is to spend an hour of time to get the ticket for "free" at a time, date, and location of agonizing inconvenience. (Typical conversation: "If you use your points for "any time" travel it will require 240,000 points for two first class tickets, but you'll have to fly out of Boston, not Providence, and change in Chicago and Denver; your departing flight will be at 6:10 am, the connections are only 42 minutes, and the airport will be closed when you arrive. Oh, yes, and you and your wife cannot sit together.")

Who needs this? Unfortunately, everything from the Division of Motor Vehicles to the electric company to Bergdorf Goodman's customer service line is starting to sound like this.

We wish, because the monoliths have made it too hard to do. Listen to me carefully, because our options may have changed.

We have priority systems which resemble a demolition derby

Remember the bumper cars at the amusement parks and carnivals? I loved them because there was no rhyme or reason other than bashing into someone else full tilt. There wasn't a race to win or a record to challenge. The idea was to participate gleefully in chaos, slamming friend and foe alike.

Too often, that's what our priorities resemble. Hit the nearest thing hard and don't worry about progress around the track.

We wish we had achieved more because we didn't realize at the time that the issue was more important than what we were actually doing: teaching the dog to say "I love you;"[6] upgrading software from version 4.06.5.3 to 4.06.5.3a; trying to program the TIVO so as not to miss one episode of *America's Got Talent*; attempting to complete the Thursday Suduko puzzle; browsing at Wal-Mart; and wishing for still more things to happen that we haven't had time to do!

Our lives are seriously out of kilter. We handle the immediate more than the urgent. We listen to volume, not reason. We are distracted by a "funny" video on TV or YouTube which was clearly staged, rather than paying attention to our retirement planning or next vacation.

---

[6] Do not laugh: A woman who worked for me on an underused employee hot line with a lot of time on her hands taught my dog, Trotsky, to say "I love you." It was clearly discernable, and my son nearly lost his lunch when he heard it. There was a woman, well, with too much time on her hands.

We're smacking what's directly in front of us as hard as we can until the ride ends. We have no idea what the point is, how you win, or when to say "Enough!"

People wish because they have become professional victims

Welcome to victimhood nation. It's not our fault and never will be. It's "them." Just ask Harvard Professor Henry Louis Gates, Jr., and Cambridge police sergeant James Crowley. At least that's one way to get a beer at the White House.

One of the great science fiction movies of all time was *Them*, an early nuclear-age, cold war horror about ants that grew to, oh, about 400,000 times normal size. It was a great premise, foreshadowing giant spiders, women, grasshoppers, snakes, and assorted other critters. It opens with a stunned little girl who survived their attack, speechless, except to scream, "THEM!!"

We wish things to happen because we've become disempowered, professional victims of "them." "They" are responsible; "they" made us do it; you can't fight "them."

Well, even the giant ants were defeated, though it required a lot of napalm. Similarly, we need to torch the belief system that would have us believe we are victims, incapable of directing our fate, unable to fight the tide of persecution.

I don't know whether or not you can "fight city hall," since city hall is a building the sentiments and motives of which I cannot discern. But I do know (having served as the chairman of a planning board in the most affluent community in the state) that you *can* fight unfair tax assessments, illegal dumping, inappropriate property use, and intrusive noise. You may not be able to change our foreign policy tomorrow, but you can participate tomorrow in electing someone whose views you believe just might. You probably can't get your boss fired for unethical, unfair, and/or bullying tactics, but you can appeal to the corporate ombudsman, human resources, or your boss's boss. (Please don't tell me that you don't want to put your job at risk, which is self-imposed victimhood. Do you really want to continue working for a firm which would take your legitimate grievance and use it against you?)

Our political parties tend to disempower us, though politicians descant at length about "the American people" and what we supposedly want (usually some good deal for them). They claim that we need large government, or strict regulation, or confiscatory taxes, or stringent product protection in order to survive. But we don't. Putting a sign on the shampoo that the product "should not be taken internally" is hardly a help to me and there is no history of millions dying in this country by mistakenly and foolhardily imbibing liquid Prell prior to the regulatory warning label. We shouldn't need a ridiculous lawsuit filed against McDonald's to force them to create advisories informing us that their coffee is hot.

I'm expecting hot coffee. Do me a favor, and warn me *if it isn't hot*, so I'll know to go someplace else.

Power does not corrupt, the good Lord Acton (who admonished us about this and "absolute power corrupting absolutely") not withstanding. *Powerlessness* corrupts. That's right, the more people believe they lack power, the more they will "invent" it, and that creates a triumph of means over ends. And that my friends, is spelled bureaucracy. ***And that starts with "B" and that rhymes with "P" and that stands for Pool!!***

Sorry, where was I?

Okay: Our perceived powerlessness in the face of regulation, monolithic organizations, uncaring institutions, and a health care system that only Rube Goldberg could love, forces us to become corrupt. Our corruption is the abandonment of systematic and methodical plans to achieve and succeed. Instead, we make excuses, amplified and encouraged by our "leaders." The people who want our votes, or our contributions to their cause, or our support for their agendas, want us to feel as if we have no power and only they can lead the way.

We *wish* because we feel we can no longer *do*; that forces beyond our poor power to influence and actually control our destiny.

The manifestations look like this:

Cheating: Everyone cheats because everyone is doing it. Why should I be at a disadvantage? Athletes use steroids. Business executives cook the books. What difference does it make if I use a stolen copy of the lieutenant's exam, or roll back my odometer, or use a sermon that is actually written by someone I heard while traveling? A friend of mine told me that his daughter, studying to be a rabbi, delivered a wonderful speech which a classmate copied and used in a term paper to get an "A." When the school authorities were confronted—*religious* school authorities—they were unsure of what punishment to mete out, but expulsion was not even considered. The apparent philosophy of the thief: "I really wish I could do that, so maybe I can cut some corners and get there, because the hard work is too intimidating and 'they' would probably stop me anyway."

Tall Poppy Syndrome: My friends in Australia, a regular haunt of mine, explain the "tall poppy syndrome" this way: Bring home a flashy, expensive new car in America and neighbors will most likely ask where you bought it, how much it is, how powerful is the engine, and what it takes to buy one. In Australia, however, that car would be scratched or otherwise damaged the next day, because the tall poppy always gets cut down. We wish for things because we feel that we'd be begrudged if we honestly went out and acquired them. In other words, it's fine to win the BMW in a raffle, but even if you can afford it, "they" would never let you live down the extravagant purchase. I wish I had it, because just going out and getting it would be uncomfortable.

Go for broke: I fall down laughing when the multi-state Powerball Lottery gets to $150 million or thereabouts. Because at that magical level, there are suddenly lines in the lottery stores, people drive from Connecticut to Rhode Island to buy tickets (there are too few of us in Rhode Island to create long lines, except at the Division of Motor

Vehicles, where the glacier-like movements of the employees make three people into a long line), and those folks who usually buy two tickets now buy twenty. What's going on here? Are you telling me that your life is such that a mere $2 million after tax is not worth getting excited about, but for $150 *very large* you throw the kids and dogs in the SUV and hunt down ducats? This is the "go for broke" mentality which is the apotheosis of wishing: "If only I could...." (Most lottery winners keep working, and a few wind up in jail, or worse. As a class, I don't view these folks as particularly happy or peaceful.)

Professional victimhood and the anomie and alienation that follow serve to create more wishful thinking and less hard work and dramatic action.

Summary: non-wishful thinking

Wishing upon a star may be a wonderful way to enjoy Disneyeseque dreams, but it's also a formula to flush your life away. The ability to Thrive is based upon the volition and talents required to plan, orchestrate, adjust, and celebrate your life.

"Wishing" has become an unconscious default position for most of us. I counsel a great many stressed people who present to me this scenario: "When she said that, I wish I had replied...." or "When he interrupted, I wish I could have said...." This "opportunity lost" creates huge stress, no matter how much venting takes place, *ex post facto*. We actually seem to place ourselves in positions of impotent wishing rather than potent action.

We wish our lives away over perceived lack of control which becomes *de facto* lack of control. We convince ourselves that we can't take action or that the action we can take is insufficient. We concern ourselves with other people and other opinions which, in reality, are irrelevant.

We don't Thrive because we connive.

CHAPTER 2

Wishing is to achievement what watching TV is to aerobic fitness

Why dreams can make you fat

We undermine ourselves by wishing things were different. We fantasize ourselves into a world of denial no less toxic than an opium den. It's no wonder that hookah bars have opened in New York.

Achievement may be relative but it's nonetheless measurable. Unlike Justice Potter Stewart's capricious definition of pornography ("I know it when I see it"), we can measure where the bar is and by how much we've missed it or cleared it. When subjectivity inevitably rears its ambiguous head, we simply look to the majority and/or the authority figures. Thus, television programs are cancelled, paintings don't sell, music isn't played.

Don't be duped by those who tell you "They just don't appreciate you." *Being appreciated is part of Thriving*, whether it's for your talent, your experience, your wit, your art, or your power. Objectively and subjectively, you can readily measure achievement and success. Whether you like Madonna or not is a matter of taste; whether she has been successful as an artist is not debatable.

Why do those lottery lines only begin to appear at the $100 million mark?

Pray tell, why is it that people don't get excited about the lottery until it reaches astronomical numbers? You can walk into any store selling lottery tickets at any time and in short order purchase tickets at the $10 million or $70 million mark, as the prize escalates.

But once it's up there around $100 million, serpentine lines emerge from mini-marts, convenience stores, and liquor shops. People from Connecticut and Massachusetts actually drive to Rhode Island (not too fast, or they miss it) where they believe the lines will be shorter.[7]

Are there actually people out there, leading middle class lives or worse, who don't feel it's worth their time to purchase a lottery ticket at ten million-to-one odds for the chance of winning, say, a cool $15 million pre-tax, but who suddenly see an entirely different *raison d'être* for getting on line to purchase tickets at 30 million to one to win $125 million? They have too many important things to do unless nine figures are in play?

People have lost perspective. The media have inured us with McMansions, super yachts, and foreign cars. But even in turbulent economies, over 90 percent of the population could live very well for many years by shepherding a $15 million windfall. After taxes, the recipient would be receiving a quarter million yearly, at least, at very low interest rates from very safe investments. Isn't it apodictic that, if you did nothing else (which most people actually would not find appealing) that's still a nice living wage?

I've had people ask me if they should allow a publication to publish their article when there was a chance that a "better" publication might come along. I've seen people agonize so long over whether they could get tickets to still a better play (or better seats to a single play), that they've missed the curtain. Weekly, I watch people miss opportunities because they are wondering whether there might be something better around the corner.

---

[7] Looking for a Ph.D. dissertation? Calculate the relative time spent waiting in line in northern Connecticut versus getting in the car, driving to southern Rhode Island, waiting in line there, and driving back. Bear in mind that Connecticut is, per capita, the wealthiest state in the union. It must be inherited money.

Publish the article, take the tickets in front of you, seize the opportunity that presents itself. You can always "fine-tune" and adjust, but get your ass in gear.

We may not want half the population lining up at every newspaper shop twice a week, stopping traffic and impeding emergency vehicles, so you may make a case that it's better for people only to become excited when the stakes are terribly high. But I would make the case to you that the stakes are as valuable *as you perceive them to be.*

For the anal-retentive amongst you, there is a formula you may want to consider in terms of perspective and what behaviors may be appropriate. You can apply it in terms of the lottery, the theater, a dinner with friends, a new job, a hobby, or anything else which requires some calculation of the input vs. the output, of the potential "return" for your real and psychic investment.

Anticipated Value = Likelihood of Improvement x Impact of Improvement

- Anticipated value: What you expect to gain by the investment/attention.[8]

- Likelihood of improvement: Your belief in the probability of success in achieving/obtaining the value.

- Impact of improvement: The actual gain in your condition/status that would result.[9]

So as you examine a venture or option or opportunity, to gain some perspective for you, personally, consider my equation. If you were to take off from work to watch your kid's soccer game, your experience might tell you that your kid would be super proud to have one of the

---

[8] Remember that real wealth is discretionary time, so the "investment" includes time, money, energy, repute, focus, priority, support, and so forth.

[9] Depending on the individual, this could include reputation, position, income, credibility, repayment of financial or non-financial debt, power, learning, and so forth.

If you play blackjack at a casino in Vegas, the chances are good that you'll be surrounded at the table by self-appointed "experts" who actually believe they can win in the long run. They follow tried and true rules which increase the odds of success, e.g., don't get hit if the dealer is showing a 6 (the dealer is more likely to "bust"); even if you have the opportunity, don't double your bet if the dealer is showing a face card (the dealer is more likely to win); and so on. They are like cultists in the Temple of Numbers.

And they are screamingly boring. They believe they are there to win, and they are disappointed if they don't win.

However, some of us are there to have fun. I will "double down" every chance I get, and I don't care if the dealer is holding an ace, a gun, and a sign that says, "Don't do that!" That's because I'm there to be entertained, and I realize that my stake for the night is the equivalent of spending money at the theater. I'm paying for entertainment, and my degree of enjoyment (and ROI) is largely dependent on my own conduct. If I actually win, that's just gravy—"found money."

Many of the cultists hate my approach, thinking that it gives them worse cards, and will often openly criticize my play. That can be intimidating, except I regard that as part of my entertainment, and I welcome it![10]

Achievement, success, gratification—they depend on your perspective and definition. Have you ever gone to a theater expecting to make money while you're there? Why would gambling be different when you know the odds are against you?

---

[10] At one table, a bejeweled and overly painted woman said, "You're ruining this for the rest of us." "Yes," I said, "I've been sent here by management to make you miserable. I also have more chips than you, which must just increase your misery."

few parents present in the middle of the day, and your relationship would be further enhanced by your show of support. The anticipated value of the likelihood and impact will more than offset the loss of an afternoon's work (don't forget, my audience usually comprises entrepreneurs), or a white lie to get out of a meeting, or just playing hooky.

However, if your kid is embarrassed for you to see him merely collecting bench splinters, and has asked you not to come, and you would be going just for yourself because you want an excuse not to work, you now have a different value equation. For an afternoon away from garrulous customers, you've set back you relationship with your progeny and Dr. Spock will haunt your dreams.

For some people, the threshold of excitement, lottery-wise, begins at $100 million, to the extent that they significantly change their behaviors and lives to act upon that incentive. I find that mindless, as misguided as those self-important people at the blackjack table expecting to win by playing "scientifically" and who look absolutely miserable as they do it. Here is a brief hierarchy of anticipated value at that blackjack table, from best to worst:

1. Winning money and being ecstatic.

2. Losing money and being ecstatic.

3. Winning money and being miserable.

4. Losing money and being miserable.

If you see playing blackjack as entertainment, you'll be in the first two positions ALL the time! If you see it as a viable attempt to come out ahead, you'll be in the bottom two positions most of the time. (Because when these people win, they immediately become apotropaic about losing next time and guarding their winnings. Meanwhile they expend all kinds of energy and angst trying to get the casino to "comp" them—give them a free room, meal, or breath mint—because they have temporarily "won.")

A final thought: In my consistently sold-out workshop, "Moving from Six Figures to Seven," part of the preparation work is to detail exactly what you would do with an extra million dollars in income, every cent of it. Over half the participants (the honest half, no doubt) candidly admit that this was the hardest question of all for them to answer. How about you? Are you seeking something for which you really have a clear purpose?

Lord Acton got it wrong about power and corruption

Here's Lord Acton's actual quote to Bishop Mandell Creighton in 1887: "Power tends to corrupt, and absolute power corrupts absolutely. Great men are almost always bad men."

Well, not really.

Power does not corrupt, although corrupt people can abuse power. I've found that most of them were, as my daughter would say, pretty "sketchy" to begin with. However, *powerlessness* corrupts pretty thoroughly and continually. Psychologically, people cannot comfortably live with the perception that they are powerless. So they make it up. That's right, they create artificial power. And there's a name for that: bureaucracy.

Bureaucracy is the triumph of means over ends. We all bemoan bureaucracy:

- The hamburger guy who tells you that the milkshakes are at the next window and, when you go there, he winds up behind that window as well.

- The Japanese customs official who tells you that you cannot use red ink on his forms (it was clearly explained to arriving Americans on the form, in Japanese) and you must fill out a new form, and go to the rear of the 30-minute line.

- The receptionist who tells you that she can connect you to voice mail, but has no way to know if someone is actually in the office at the moment, and cannot, herself, take messages.

- The motor vehicles clerk who tells you that you must have a social security card to get a replacement license, and while she knows that you must have a license to get a replacement social security card, that's really not her problem.

- FedEx in the U.S. assuring that luggage can be shipped to Australia, but the Australia FedEx operation returning it because they refuse to accept luggage shipped from the U.S.[11]

And yet....we all engage in a variety of bureaucratic habits in our pursuits. You don't believe me? How many "friends" do you have who:

- Brag that they drive 20 minutes to save five cents a gallon on gas? That's less than two dollars per tank, never mind the distance it takes to get there and back and 40 minutes of your, er, your friend's time.

- Finish a deplorable book because they've started it, and they refuse not to finish it, even if it's *The Electric Fork Chronicles.*

- Insist on following a rigid routine, such as reading the newspapers only at certain times, or taking the garbage out in certain clothes, or going through certain rituals before driving the car or mowing the lawn?

- Meticulously spend an hour reconciling bank statements, even though the most it's ever off is a few dollars and it's simpler to merely take the bank's word for it and make the adjustment, rather than spend all that time and frustration trying to justify the bank's main computer's solution?

---

[11] As you no doubt have surmised, yes, variations of all of these have happened to me.

- Insist on just dumb rules and/or adhere to them? You can tear that tag off your mattress that threatens you with legal ruin if you try it. It's nonsensical to insist that kids stand in straight lines by size order.[12]

When people don't have real power they make it up (fill out the form again and get to the back of the line), or they create regimens which make sense only to their own sense of self-identify (I read the newspaper at 5:30, could we talk at 6:30?). The key, therefore, is to empower ourselves.

Now, "empowerment" has become a buzzword of dubious worth, so let me define what I mean by it here:

Empowerment is the ability to make decisions that influence your life and/or the outcomes of your work.

It's that simple and that difficult. (I used to tell people that my wife and I were married so long because she made the small decisions and allowed me to make the major decisions. Thus, she decided where we lived, the kids' schools, the cars we drove, and so on. I decided about world peace, tax rates, and climate change. I stopped telling people this one day when my wife overheard me.)

I don't stand in lines, or endure long holding times on the phone. I take control of my life. I find alternative means. That may mean paying somewhat more to have a concierge get me tickets, or using a membership because the auto club can replace my license with no waiting, or emailing an executive who I can find online instead of putting up with the black holes of customer service lines. (If the calls are recorded for training purposes, why doesn't the service ever improve?)

---

[12] I estimate that approximately 4,000,000 recreational hours were lost between 1946 and 1976 due to irrational adherence to staying out of the water for an hour after eating. This later turned out to be a worthless precaution (to prevent cramps), but the otherwise mature adults saying, "It's only 52 minutes, give it more time," to rational and frustrated youth is one of the bureaucratic milestones of our time.

The more you are disempowered at work combined with the less you empower yourself personally, the more likely you will be frustrated, angry, and even depressed. For those of you in your own business, that disempowerment at work can still happen, even though you know the boss so well. The customer is *not* always right: The customer is often a pain in the ass who needs to be fired. (Whoever created that bromide had to have been one of these customers who buys something, wears it to an event, and then returns it.) The Cross Pen Company once replaced a pen for free which the owner had dropped into his lawn mower. Nordstrom once took merchandise back they hadn't sold (or had perspiration stains under the arms). I don't call that super service. I call that excruciatingly stupid management, how about you?

Similarly, if you agree to be on a fundraising committee and you hate fundraising, you've allowed yourself to be disempowered. Not surprisingly, but incredibly uncomfortably, this applies to family, as well. If you totally sacrifice your time and interests to your children, you will grow to despise them. (My God, did he really just say that?!) Raising your kids well doesn't mean that they take priority over all else. (He did just say that!) It means that you must be happy and successful yourself to convey that happiness and success to your little DNA perpetuators. (He does make sense about that.)

It's about putting your own oxygen mask on first. Many of us traveled extensively during the little darlings' formative years, but continued to contribute to their development and spend quality time with them. So, how is it possible to be a good parent even when you're in Hong Kong, but a bad parent when you deny them your time when you're at home but doing something for yourself? It's not distance, it's personal need and fulfillment. No one would suggest that everyone stop traveling to stay home more with the kids. Why would anyone suggest you drop everything you're doing just because you happen to be in the next room?[13]

---

[13] I bought my first Ferarri in 1995 when both my kids had gone to college and I had a combined tuition bill of $50,000 a semester. This way, I didn't resent them!

One of the worst crimes against your own humanity is disempowering yourself. That means that you willingly allow decisions which influence your life to be taken from you, or refuse to make them. Examples abound:

- You put up with a job or boss that makes your life miserable. (Almost all people leave their boss, not their job, by the way. That's a lesson I've tried to teach corporate clients with uneven success.)

- You are involved in a damaged or damaging relationship which you do not take the initiative to either fix or abandon. (Any psychologist worth her diploma will tell you that self-esteem is largely a function of creating and maintaining healthy personal relationships.)

- You become fearful to "pull the trigger" and make an investment, or sell a property, or commit to a vacation. You become obsessed with the belief that there may be something better and you need to wait. (There well may be something better, but at what cost and what time? Life is about success, not perfection.)

- You allow guilt and baggage to impede your decision making. After all, how can you dance when your parents told you repeatedly you were clumsy? How can you consider an advanced degree at your age when your friends told you that it's so much harder to learn when the brain resembles a pomegranite? ("Dropping baggage" is not the answer, because it's still on the train, going with you at the same speed. You have to throw it off the train into the countryside, and if it kills a cow or two, you'll just have to live with that.)

"Empowerment" means something. You need to make it mean something for you, or else someone or something else is running your life.

My favorite country song title is, "If I had shot her when I wanted to, I would have been out by now"

And my favorite book title is, *Get Your Tongue Out of My Mouth, I'm Kissing You Goodbye* (by Cynthia Heimel). But I digress.

We tend to look back at our lives bemoaning what we should have done. I call this "the view of the wake," since we are looking back where the boat has already sailed (and it might as well refer to a wake where one views a deceased body—metaphorically, your own). My father-in-law unfailingly pointed out the land supporting various shopping malls, athletic facilities, condominium developments, and major casinos which he could have "bought for a song" when he was younger. Yes, and I could have made a fortune on Microsoft had I:

- Anticipated the digital revolution.

- Known Bill Gates.

- Appreciated that he wasn't demented but actually had a new idea.

- Had any disposable money at all to invest.

Yes, we should have studied Mandarin in high school, paid more attention to English Lit in college instead of getting blitzed and trying to score at parties, told our first boss that we were out of there in the morning, never married our first spouse, had kids sooner or later, dared to buy that home/boat/car/work of art when it would have been less of a risk, and so on. Second guessing ourselves ought to be an Olympic event. (On the BBC: "Her momentum is good, she's well into her regrets right after college, but she's neglected both her weight and her bad hair cuts and I believe that will cost her with the Romanian judge.")

Life does not plot against you. You are not in a feculent maze created by a berserk English lord trying to lure enough dumb tourists to pay for the upkeep on his ancestral home in Chapthighs-Under-Tweed.

The trouble when you stare at the wake is that you fail to see the new opportunities appearing constantly through the windshield (or whatever you look through on a boat).

There is a plethora of analogous opportunities facing you, but you have to take the time to identify, appreciate, and pursue them, no less than one would have had to do to appreciate Bill Gates, or Apple, or low-fare airlines, or washboard abs decades ago.

You have a personal accountability to look for opportunities that can enhance your life, work, interests, and relationships. That accountability is going to be nearly impossible to live up to if you:

- Are locked into a regimen of habits and procedures.

- Hang out with negative, demeaning, or dumb people.

- Are afraid to try new experiences.[14]

- Bemoan your past instead of become excited about your future.

- Refuse to learn or are threatened by learning.

- Get your information from Twitter and Tony the bartender.

A corollary to "only if" is "wishing." I wish I had said this to him when I had the chance; I wish I didn't have such bad skin; I wish that I had traveled more in college; I wish that I could eat that awful looking sushi and be cool. This is where you wish your life away. If we spent as much time planning and seeking opportunity as we did wishing that we had done things differently, we'd all be in much better shape.

---

[14] If you have an allergy to fish, fine, I don't expect you to throw yourself under the boat, but otherwise put the piece of sushi in your mouth and stop complaining about how it looks. You probably don't look so hot to a tuna, either.

Here is a frightening little equation for you to calculate in the privacy of this book:

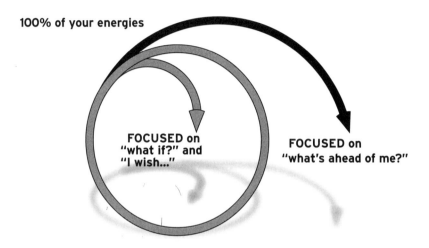

100% of your energies

FOCUSED on "what if?" and "I wish…"

FOCUSED on "what's ahead of me?"

Where is your effort going?

So: If we agree that you only have 100 percent of your energy available at the best of times (I have no idea what motivational speakers or irrational bosses mean when they say, "Give me 110 percent," except that they hadn't done well in school), then the question is, "How is it allocated?" Are you inside the circle (your own head) or out in the world?

How much of your energy devoted to these two dynamics is apportioned to each? Do you spend half the time regretting the "what ifs" and half the time saying, "I wonder if…."? Or are you immersed and submerged within that circle of *ex post facto* regret?

My experiences are that most people spend upwards of 60 percent of their time in the confines of the circle, and for many it's far worse than that. Now, ask yourself this question: "If I changed just 10 or 15 percent of the focus of my energy from inside that circle to outside the circle, what would the subsequent benefit be to my self-worth, my innovation, my assertiveness, and my success?"

I'll tell you what it would be: substantial and significant. Just as it's never too late to derive the health benefits of quitting smoking or becoming sober, it's never too late to move your focus to the "What should I do?" and away from the "What have I done?" If you're at 75/25, you can certainly move to 60/40. At 50/50, you can "tilt the balance" to the positive. But even at 30/70, you can nevertheless derive huge results from moving to 15/85, because you're always shifting available, expendable energy from a negative pursuit to a positive pursuit. Instead of wishing your life away, you're examining your future. Instead of bemoaning "What if?" you're assessing "Why not?"

Since positive relationships contribute so much to positive self-esteem, I want to take a few minutes to examine the phenomenon above in terms of personal relationships. What happens when you:

- Tell your partner, "What if you hadn't accepted that invitation without asking me, the night we had the accident?"

- Tell your child, "I wish you hadn't alienated your teacher during the very first day of class."

- Tell a sibling, "If they had listened to me years ago, we wouldn't have to pay for their upkeep today."

- Tell a good friend, "I wish I could help you, but I don't see any way that I can."

We not only wish away our lives and stare backwards at them over the stern, we damage relationships, often subliminally and unconsciously, by treating them with the same backward-looking and regretful attitude. What we should be saying is:

- "Let's talk about some alternatives for transportation while the car is repaired."

- "I think I know some ways to bring your teacher around, and I'm certainly happy to talk to the teacher myself."

- "It's fortunate we're in a position to help, how do you think we should absorb the costs?"

- "While I can't help you financially, I can introduce you to some contacts who may be quite supportive, and I can help with the publicity."

Every day there are new opportunities for growth and prosperity. (The motivational speaking industry is rife with people who make a living merely demonstrating that they have overcome far more adversity than you need to, and they are fine and successful. But I don't cotton to that approach. No one has ever progressed much just because someone else has come from farther down, or merely due to the fact that they are better off than others by comparison.[15]) But you have to be looking, literally, *forward* to them, and not wasting time and energy looking backwards or bemoaning things that can't be changed anyway.

Thus, you must start engaging in "forward-thinking talk." The way we talk to ourselves informs our behavior. Negative talk—the "wishing" and "what if" and "woe is me"—is the equivalent of the packing peanuts amongst the baggage that we're carrying around with us. The baggage needs to be thrown off the train, but sometimes the packing material falls out and clings to us.

You can't afford to talk to yourself or anyone else in terms of "If only" and "I wish I had." That's like watching the rerun of a sporting event and hoping that it turns out differently the second time. You can't change your personal history, but you can prevent it from ruining your future.

---

[15] *It has not yet been recorded that any human being has gained a very large or permanent contentment from meditation upon the fact that he is better off than others.* — Sinclair Lewis

If you want to lose weight, stop eating so much

Over the past 20 years Americans alone have probably spent in excess of $40 billion on weight loss: diets, special foods, health clubs, equipment, counseling, surgery, sports, and all sorts of paraphernalia. (Have you ever seen a "Thighmaster"? Looks like an extraterrestrial nut cracker.)

Yet Americans are fatter than ever.

We'd rather deal with the easy stuff—buying equipment, engaging in brief diets, hiring a trainer—than the hard stuff—stop eating so much. An "all you can eat buffet" is to dining what a mud fight is to dancing. We have become obsessed with fat and sugar (deadly in combination, because they encourage further eating) and portions that require two people to lift. ("Hi, I'm Jason and I'll be your server today. This is Henry, and he'll be helping you lift the food through the first three courses, when he will then go on break.")

My mother used to tell me as a youngster and finicky eater that (now this is only a few years after World War II), "There are people in Europe starving, eat that!" Well, today, she would have been fairly accurate since, if people were starving in Europe, any of these seven-course dinners over three hours could have probably taken care of several countries' needs.

- If you want to lose weight, stop stuffing your face.
- If you want to influence others at meetings, stop being too intimidated to speak.
- If you want to make more money, stop working for such low wages.
- If you want to spend more time with your kids, stop spending it on other things.
- If you want to dance better, stop avoiding lessons.

- If you want to drive a better car, stop spending your money on other things.

- If you don't like your boss, stop working there.

You get the picture. If you want to Thrive, then you have to stop doing things that are anti-Thrive. You can't trick yourself by trodding over hot chestnuts, or listening to motivational tapes, or repeating affirmations ("I AM a sumo wrestler, I AM a sumo wrestler...."), or putting hexes on other people.

This is why dreams can make you fat.

We are largely in control of our own destinies. Oh, we can't choose to live to 160, or to become multi-zillionaires, or to star in motion pictures. But we can extend out lives through healthy habits, we can extend our fortune through intelligent careers, and we can promote ourselves through selfless service and dedication. When I was skiing a couple of times a year, I learned a fascinating fact: The view is spectacular from the side of the mountain. You don't have to be at the very top. And if coming back down on a double black diamond is the only route from the very top, then you tend to become very contented with the view from lower altitudes surrounding the blue rectangles.

Wishing, like talk, is cheap. You can't wish yourself success or your enemy failure. You can't wish for a replay or a mulligan. You can't wish for a shortcut.

Now, you may tell me you *can* wish if you like, because you are able to do so. But I'm telling you that you shouldn't because you're wasting your time and energy. You can wish all you want, but you'll be wishing your life away. If you want to look toward the future instead of living mired in the past, you can't afford to wish. You just don't have the time or energy to spare.

If you really seek to lose weight, then eat less and exercise more. You're in control of that equation, whether you're traveling or at home, with friends or alone, happy or sad. Losing weight has to be important enough to be beyond mere wishing. So does earning more money, repairing a relationship, and organizing your life.

You may wish someone a happy birthday, or provide best wishes for a marriage or new job. But everyone is better served if you provide a nice gift or a character reference.

John Kennedy didn't say he wished to go to the moon. He said we will go to the moon. And he got it done a half century ago with near-primitive technology.

Stop wishing. Start acting. Reach for the stars.

CHAPTER 3

Somewhere over the rainbow.... are tons of bluebird droppings

Happy little bluebirds can fly because they have wings!

We long for an idealized future, and use metaphor in place of thought. What does the "war on terror" really mean? What is actually "over the rainbow"?

And our best apothegms contradict each other nicely: Haste makes waste, but a stitch in time saves nine. Our reach should exceed our grasp, but prudent risk is best. Seek and ye shall find, but opportunity is always knocking.

I like Damon Runyon the best: "The race is not always to the swift or the battle to the strong....but that's the way to bet."

The grass isn't greener, it's simply not *your* grass

When we were kids, living in the inner city amongst four- and five-story "apartment buildings," we managed to get into the tiny back-yards, courtyards, and alleys by scaling fences and knocking holes in wooden fences. We did this simply to get into the next bit of open space, even though it was often uglier and more cramped than where we came from.

No matter, it represented something "foreign," and forbidden, and even fatalistic: We overcame snarling, teeth-bearing dogs (one, famous-ly called Mikey, a big Collie, actually nipped at us escaping over the fence; we didn't sue in those days, we cried), rusted picket fences six feet high for which a tetanus shot wouldn't have even been vaguely effective, and threatening tenants who would not hesitate to throw a rock or beer can or even a lamp.

We did this because we wanted to *go* there. It seemed to make sense at the time. In retrospect, I wonder what I was thinking and why I wasn't killed. (I can still see Mikey perfectly.)

We choose to disguise reality. That's good and bad, depending. For example, we feel that "other" families get along better, that no one else has our silly fears, or that surely no one has ever had a moment as embarrassing as the one we recently endured. Let me assure you that's a preposterous belief system. Even the President of the United States, Michelle Pfeiffer, Jack Welch, Meryl Streep, Prince Charles, and Nelson Mandela have passed gas at inappropriate times, been caught with their hand someplace it shouldn't have properly been, and have given lousy advice or poor performances.

Not one of us is perfect, we are all sinners and error-prone, and we have to stop acting as if others have some secret decoder ring which enables them to figure out what the rest of us can't.

On the other hand (as the economists are fond of intoning), it is fine to synthesize and alchemize happiness. I once thought that it was absurd rationalizing to create false happiness, as in, "Losing that job the same week that my wife left me was the best thing to ever happen to me." A Harvard psychologist, Dan Gilbert, has actually found that people who engage in such synthesized happiness are healthier and truly happier than those who wait for empirical euphoria—the race won, the prize taken home, the accolades from the crowd.

So disguising reality ain't all bad. It depends how you use the subterfuge.

The grass, after all, may really *be* greener, or you may just convince yourself that it is, or you may get your jollies just from trying to find out.

The key is to avoid being in a place where you can't win enough, or be successful enough, or be happy enough. You can't compare yourself to others, or to some arbitrary standards, or even to your own past performance (we all age, Bunky). You need the self-mastery to inform yourself that you are doing well, you are succeeding, and you are happy, without needing to validate those conclusions against anyone else's standards and practices.

Happiness is personal.

How can you tell if you're pursuing greener pastures out of pleasure, or a sense of obligation, or a fear of not doing so, or some other crazy metaphoric meaning ("Don't go gently into that good night...")? Ask yourself these questions, but not out loud if you're in a public place:

1. Do I try new things out of a sense of experimentation and curiosity, or out of fear and obligation?

2. Can I create a learning experience, a good feeling, a lesson learned from most of my new undertakings?

3. Do I use my own metrics for success or do I rely on the approbation of others?

4. Can I find a bright light, or at least a burning ember, even in events that disappoint me or fail to meet my expectations?

5. Do I accept qualitative differences or do I make arbitrary "rulings" on what's better or best? (Example: You can enjoy the speed and athleticism of a basketball game, and the aesthetic beauty of a classic art exhibition, without having to compare the two.)

6. You tend to see setbacks, even disappointments, but not failures.

7. You realize that success is wonderful on your own terms, but it's never permanent, and only leads to further opportunities and challenges.

8. You can infect other people with your sense of wonder, fulfillment, and joy.

The grass isn't always greener, it's just *other* grass.

You have the ability to create your own happiness, whether or not it is empirically validated by others or merely subjectively rationalized by yourself. The point is, you should be happy in your own yard, happy in the next yard, and happy visualizing still other yards. That's because life isn't about black and white choices.

Life is a rheostat, not an "on/off" switch

A great obstacle to Thriving is the "on/off" quandary. People are constantly placing themselves in front of metaphysical doors, believing that they can walk through only one and the other is lost forever.

I have news for you, you can open both doors, take a gander inside, and even go in and dance around a bit to see if you like the music. We have dynamic choices, not static alternatives.

Should we go to the beach or to the mountains? Why not go to both, just figure out how. Do I take a tough stance with the boss, or try to be conciliatory? Why not reserve both prerogatives, and see how the conversation goes? Should I surprise her with the present in the morning, alone, or later when the entire family is here? Why not give her two presents?

You can set a rheostat to the light level, or temperature level, or volume level that you prefer at the moment. You can always change it. You can be fairly precise in determining the result.

You can do the same with most of your life. I know that you may believe that you only have enough money for a single vacation, or solely one opportunity to impress a client, or a choice between two lovers (I dimly remember a song about that). But that's because you've undermined yourself with "either/or," "go/no go," "on/off" thinking.

If you picture a continuum for virtually any scale, you'll find some interesting options. First, true aberrant behavior is off the ends of the scale. Second, on the scale, you have options. Suppose this line represents "assertiveness," with the left being low on the scale and the right being high:

ASSERTIVENESS

If you are off the left margin, then you are in a coma, and if you are outside of the right margin, you are warlike and belligerent. But other than that, there are no value judgments for "normal" behavior.[16] That is, neither high nor low assertiveness are inherently good or bad. *Either is subject to the situation, the performer, and the others present.*

While you may have a "home base" on here that is more comfortable than other places for you, you also have the ability to travel across the continuum. Thus, the rheostat:

- When you are at home you may (and probably should) choose to be far less assertive than at work (though even here there may be exceptions for a child's punishment or a neighbor's intransigence).

---

[16] This is a variant of Social Style Theory. My favorite book on the subject is *Management Style/Social Style*, by Robert and Dorothy Bolton (AMACOM, 1984).

- You may be somewhat less assertive with a key client's some-what unreasonable demands than a co-workers unreasonable demands, since you don't fear alienating the co-worker as much as you do the key client.

- You may be more or less assertive depending where that "home base" is, because that will be your default position, given your nurturing, experiences, and the DNA coursing through your veins.

If you want to Thrive, you must provide yourself with more options. Bizarrely, perhaps, you can do this instantly by ceasing the habit of precluding your options with a "go/no go" mentality. Ask yourself these questions:

- Can I create or reassign more resources so that I can take advantage of more than one option?

- Can I combine options?

- Can I avail myself of more options by changing the timing or the sequence?

- Do I create inflexible positions in advance, or do I give myself permission to change as conditions warrant?

- Do I judge my success by implementing a certain plan, *regardless of results*, or do I measure myself on the outcomes?

- Do I take pride in making adjustments, in mid-stream corrections, and in fine-tuning?

The most successful people I encounter have the ability to be "light on their feet," to adapt to changing circumstances, and to go quickly to "Plan B"....or "C" or "D" as the situation demands.

- We were in the theater not long ago, packed for a popular performance, and four latecomers were ushered to their seats, which were not exactly to their liking (it's a 600-seat theater with good views for all over). They reversed course and left in a huff. A discernable huff.

- NASA officials refused to listen to warnings about dangerous "O-rings," and insisted that the Challenger space shuttle take off as planned.

- Steve Jobs has a string of failures to match his successes at Apple. There is the iPod, but there was also Lisa. When the now-ubiquitous iPhone met some price resistance, he lowered the price substantially, and offered credits to prior buyers.

- I facilitate (barely) a "Million Dollar Club" that I created two years ago. I told the fellow who suggested it, Rob Nixon, a charter member from Australia, that it would never work, but he insisted, and I realized I could certainly try one and see what happens. It's still happening. (Spouses attend, and my wife pointed out that over the course of a three-day meeting, she never once heard any member say, "Yes, but...." Only rheostats in this group.)

You can't go through life thinking "either, or." You can't delimit your options and possibilities. People who Thrive do so because they are able to *retain*—not *create*, but *retain*—more options for themselves, more possibilities, more potential. They tend to see wider vistas, more alternatives, fewer constraints. They are purblind to arbitrary restriction.

You don't need to create opportunity, but rather to identify and exploit what's already all around you, a much easier undertaking.

Only miserable people insist on telling you all about themselves

I understand that some people are naturally garrulous and expressive, and quickly move to create amicable relationships. I understand that you're trying to "break the ice," or make me comfortable, or appear to be friendly.

Or are you just miserable and lonely and seize the opportunity to monopolize someone else's oxygen?

I'm giving a "bye" here to those who are genuinely interested in their companion human beings and who are sincerely happy to use a verbal machete to chop down shy vines and reticent undergrowth. I'm giving you the benefit of the doubt.

But the energy suckers are something else.[17]

There is no need to inflict your life story on other people. I resent it. Unless I ask about your antecedents, or illnesses, or close escape from a Yeti, why am I constrained to listen to it? My observation is that people with very little self-fulfillment attempt to fulfill themselves by overwhelming others with their oral memoirs. (If you don't believe that, visit Facebook.)

The most devastating subject matter, in no particular order, would include:

- Family trips and celebrations.

- Illnesses, sicknesses, operations, and general unwellness.

- Children.

- Grandchildren.

- Arts recommendations, from soap operas to Baroque music.

---

[17] I learned of this term from an otherwise execrably horrible book, called *The Celestine Prophecy*, originally sold from the trunk of the author's car where, inexplicably, it didn't remain in company with the spare tire. But my gaining this single insight demonstrates that you can almost always find worth in any activity, even if, in this case, just barely.

- Directions to get somewhere.
- Lessons in how to do something, especially technological.
- Anything at all to do with any aspect of golf.
- Parents.
- Grandparents.
- Vacation trips.
- Discount options and free upgrades.
- Recreational recommendations, especially those involving all the food you can eat.
- Political opinions.
- Personal dalliances, indiscretions, and embarrassments.
- Cooking and food preparation.
- Bodily functions, no matter whose.
- Conspiracy theories of any kind.

That's my short list. Remember, I don't oppose debate and discussion, even on these topics, but I ask that I not be drowned in them, unable to breathe because the other person, with drink in hand or finger in my face, is bombarding me with recollections, remonstrance, and recommendations.

My advice to you is to eliminate these people from your lives. Thriving can be undermined by those who seek to ameliorate their misery by erupting all over you with real and imagined elements of their lonely lives. (I know this sounds harsh, but there are people who gladly will fill in the void left by our departure. They readily listen to anyone who pays. They are called "therapists," and they are paid to do so, though I don't believe nearly enough.)

I was walking on the grounds of Texaco, a mutual client, with a colleague named Mike Robert, many years ago. Mike encountered a Texaco mid-level manager, who asked if we had heard about a positive comment made about him by the CEO. We had not.

He went on to extensively recreate the scene and lavish the aforesaid praise upon himself all over again. (He also used answering machine messages that might say, "I can't come to the phone because I'm one of only 100 people in Greater New York City to be invited to a symposium on effluent management by the third deputy mayor for sewerage and offal.")

When he finally finished his self-congratulatory tale, he wandered off to find someone else to tell, having used up about 15 minutes of our time on earth. As we gasped for air, Mike observed, "A typical über-expressive. If no one applauds him, he applauds himself." Yes, but why couldn't he do it in his own room? Who allowed him to roam the property?

Learn to move away, to avoid, to circumnavigate, to run fast. If you're trapped, then use the language appropriately:

- "I'm sorry, but I have an important call to make."
- "Maybe another time, my wife (husband/significant other/kids/ yoga master/dominatrix) is waiting for me."
- "Yes, you've told me this before, and you've caught me at a time when I must find a rest room."
- "I just remembered that I haven't fed the dogs."
- "I'm feeling nauseous, do you have a handkerchief?"

- "Do I look flushed? I'm just back from Guadalupe where they've reported a deadly black mold epidemic."

- "I'm sorry, but this doesn't interest me."

The last is tough, but it's also quite true, and you may not have a dog or recently returned from hazardous places.

If you want to Thrive, you can't tolerate people who will use up your energy and resources while trying to transfuse themselves on your spirit.

"Expertise" is more than a briefcase and a plane ticket, and is never an infomercial

To be an object of interest to others, you must demonstrate and manifest expertise. As opposed to the sheer oral hurling described above, this is an expertise that others seek out and appreciate.

Think of the people to whom you've been drawn over the course of your life, particularly as you've matured and gained sophistication (as opposed to the eccentric college professor tap dancing in front of impressionable undergraduates, or the banal and insipid "motivational speaker" uttering truisms and clichés). What have they had in common? I think at least a portion of the following:

- A track record of unqualified success that validates their expertise.

- Superb use of language, including metaphor, simile, analogy, alliteration, and trochee.

- A willingness to share, but in proportion and when asked, never reaching boasting. (They tell what others need to know, not everything that they, themselves know, which is the downfall of most public speakers and professors.)

- New ideas, initiatives, and intelligence, the equivalent of intellectual property. They can combine history, geography, biography, and current events to make a telling point. (One of the greatest practitioners of this trait is the columnist and television political commentator, George Will.)

- A recognition factor, albeit perhaps in a niche or locale, which provides validation that the person is considered an expert.

- An intent to listen to opposing view and amend one's own view when facts or circumstances demand a different analysis or conclusion.

People who wish to be seen as possessing expertise—as being objects of interest, no less worth contemplating than an *object d'art*, take leadership positions. They aren't afraid to brace in the strong winds of persiflage and psychobabble. They withstand the *ad homimem* attacks ("too old," "poor background," "not with it," "can't adapt," "thinks like a man," "thinks like a woman," "too insensitive").

If you want to Thrive, you must be seen as an object of interest, as someone possessing expertise, as someone who isn't wishing upon a rainbow but rather knows why a rainbow exists.

A friend described a scene at a Washington, DC, event he attended. Robert Redford was also in attendance and, as soon as he was identified, a crowd engulfed him until he nearly disappeared from sight. Somewhat later, Ted Kennedy entered the room and, as a school of fish following an unseen signal, the crowd turned as one and reformed around the Senator. Ted Kennedy's combination of family history, charisma, political power, wealth, and smarts made him a dominating object of interest.

You want the school of fish to circle around you. It's not difficult. You merely need to acquire the attributes and traits above (assuming that marrying a Kennedy is out of the question).

On a trip to Cancun, I went on a snorkeling trip with a dozen strangers. Our boat took about 30 minutes to get on site, and one of the two leaders took us on a very long excursion. (They don't exactly have stringent rules in Cancun. In fact, no one was even asked if they could swim.) After 45 minutes of non-stop movement, we returned to the boat. We were offered the chance to dive around the boat for another half hour if we wished, on our own.

Most people were too exhausted (as was I, but when would I do this again?) and as I went overboard, one of the leaders handed me the bottle they had been using to attract fish. It was filled with some kind of alluring mystery, because the fish overwhelmed us.

I was shocked to see it had been a Coke® bottle in its former life before becoming a fish siren. As I squeezed out the strange contents, I was surrounded by hundreds of exotic fish, looking in my mask, trying to get to the bottle, eating every morsel expelled, and allowing me to actually pet and handle them.

When my supply was exhausted, the fish disappeared in a nano-second, and I returned to the boat, happy as a clam.[18] I asked one of the guides what the food consisted of, expecting some combination of algae, nutrient, and piscine steroid.

"*Estan tacos*," he told me.

Shredded tacos had made me the fish *roi de soleil*. Sometimes it's easier to be an object of interest than you might think. It's merely a matter of having the right stuff for the right audience.

---

[18] I do not know the etymology of this phrase, but its marine connotation pleases me here. (It may be because clams seem to have a smile where shell meets shell, or because high tide was clam heaven, free from predators and surrounded by food.)

If you're over 30 and not an object of interest on some matters to some people some of the time, then what have you been doing with your life?

In your business, hobbies, sporting endeavors, travels, education, or serendipity, how is it that you haven't gained enough traction to be appealing in some niche, valley or dale?

It may be because you've been skimming the surface, or not observing and listening, or not building connections and conclusions, or not focusing on doing a few things really well. (You're always better off moving three things forward a mile than a hundred things forward an inch.)

Of course, another possibility is that you've been in the company, voluntarily or not, of the survivors, not the Thrivers. You can't develop expertise attractive to others when you are always listening to others, besieged by others, and directed by others. Nor are you apt to be motivated to develop expertise when those around you are busy commiserating about why things are awful, what they "should have" ("I wish...") done, and the opportunities they've missed.

Get out from under. Start feeding the fish.

Why second and third marriages have a higher failure rate than first marriages (which already have a high failure rate[19])

You would think that a divorce would teach us a thing or two, such as the traits least desirable in a mate, the table manners we abhor, the bodily functions which should be kept from the public.

We are stunned by the failure rate of first marriages—and just think of the unofficial failure rate represented by separation and/or people living together with no love but too beaten down to do anything about

---

[19] And I'm not even talking about people co-habitating and in exclusive relationships. The failure rate of those, of which we have little data but a great deal of subjective insight, is rather astronomical. It's a Carl Saganism: "Millions and millions."

it—and we might too readily chalk that up to foolish and impetuous youth. Malcolm Gladwell might write an entire book on this, researching it and demonstrating the unknown factors that account for accidentally successful mating.

I'm not that deep.

But I will offer this for your consideration: It's not youth, because people are marrying later in life than ever before, which means, according to the church of co-habitation before marriage, that they should have achieved some semblance of contentment in the relationship or realized it was brown shoes with a blue suit. Yet the rate climbs.

Extrapolating the obvious (for which most good consultants are paid small fortunes), a second or third marriage (or exclusive relationships) should have the enormous benefit of avoiding past mistakes of choice and ignorance and capitalizing on the past successes and attraction. In other words, yes, find someone who is self-sufficient and preferably from an Eastern European fortune, but no, don't accept someone who beats the hell out of you emotionally.

Yet the divorce rate for first marriages is currently 41 percent, for second marriages 67 percent, and for third marriages 74 percent. (As noted, my understanding is that the percentages are as bad or worse for people living together or in exclusive dating arrangements.)

Why? *Because we keep choosing the same person over and over again.*

That's right, we don't learn from our past experience or performance. We are caught in a tropism leading to the exact same mate, straight and gay alike.

No one Thrives by making the same mistake over and over again, or by assuming that the one you've already made is inescapable. Even the Bible suggests that while we should forgive those who have hurt us we are under no obligation to allow them to continue to hurt us.

Or to choose others who will similarly hurt us.

DIGRESSION

We were at my wife's 25th college reunion, and I had known many of her classmates since we dated through college[20], though at different schools. At one point, a woman whose wedding we had attended, whom I'll call Ronnie, arrived, alone and dressed to the gills. She was still a very attractive, voluptuous woman.

She had been divorced for a year, her kids were grown, and she told us she had come hoping to find a man. After dinner, my wife made those subliminal wife-to-husband telepathic communications that NASA should study: "Dance with Ronnie!"

Understand that I'm not much of a dancer, though I am a practicing heterosexual and I can hold an attractive woman in my arms and sway to music. And that's exactly what I was doing, but in total silence, and I desperately realized I ought to start a conversation.

So, I said into Ronnie's very provocative ear, "How are you doing?" I am a master of sophisticated repartee.

She interpreted this as "post-divorce 'doing'," and responded, "I'm still getting over it. It's only been a year."

"How long were you married?" I stumbled on.

"Twenty-four years," she replied.

Then I lapsed into my consultant's style of inquiry and blurted, "When did you know it was wrong?"

And then, incredibly: "During the first year. But I couldn't disappoint my parents and not give them grandchildren, and the kids deserved a proper home with two parents. So, I soldiered on."

And there, on the dance floor, into Ronnie's hair, I wept.

---

[20] And were engaged our senior year with a ring purchased through my working for the postal service, and married right out of undergraduate school, as we did in those days, at age 22. No one knows that we actually eloped before graduation since my status in the Viet Nam draft was tenuous, and I'm wondering if my kids will ever read this footnote. And here we are, married for 41 years at this writing.

We have to approach life with a titration mentality. That is, distill out what does not work for you and retain what does. The idea of "necessary evil" is fostered by those too lazy or too guilty to expel the evil in their lives. It's not heroic to live with someone with whom you share no love, or, worse, who torments you emotionally or physically or spiritually. It is psychotic and pathetic. It is not strong, it is weak. It is not an example of will power, it is an example of a personality disorder.

When I served on the board of a shelter for battered women, I found (as many psychology books warned me) that battering transcends economic and educational demographics. Wealthy, smart women were battered and allowed themselves to be, every bit as much as poor, uneducated women. This is not a class crime, but a general abomination.

Stunningly, battering takes place over long periods of time because the battered party (female or male) doesn't leave. They keep returning *because they think it's their fault, that they caused it, that if they just give their partner another chance, that they can't leave the children....*

Bad personal relationships are all about battery, whether mild or strong, random or incessant, verbal or physical. If you want to Thrive, you have to fix them (very unlikely) or escape them (actually quite simple, considering the alternative).

To end on a positive, if you have a good relationship (and we're talking, as always, about success, not perfection), then you should rejoice in it, "exploit" it, and rely on it for your power, stability, and even grace.

There is nothing as central to Thriving as love and intimacy. If you don't have it, find it. Life is short. If you do have it, rejoice in it. Life is short.

CHAPTER 4

Overcoming fear of failure

And no dumb affirmations allowed

S ome things are too good to be true and some things are too true to be good.

We fail to Thrive not because we fail, but because we don't fail. If you're not failing, you're not trying. As we'll see a bit later, failure is seldom fatal. It's not the failure that thwarts our success; it's the *fear of failure*. In my son's vernacular, as a five-year-old: "I'm not afraid of the dark, I'm afraid of what might *be* in the dark."

My son got over that before he was 10. Many of you are still burdened by it.

If it looks too good to be true, let someone else try it first

While consulting with Hewlett-Packard for 10 years, it occurred to me that they were seldom first into a market, but rather a strong second, once they had evaluated what was happening. But they didn't merely follow, they innovated from there.

Similarly, Steve Jobs has consistently proclaimed that Apple jumps on "the next big thing." They don't create the next big thing, but they try to recombine and reconfigure technologies to exploit and dominate the next big thing. Hence, the amazing success of the iPod® and iPhone®. (The iPhone is an example of what I call REV: Reciprocating Exponential Value. The more iPhones, the more apps become valuable; the more apps, the more the iPhone becomes valuable; the more valuable the apps, the more people become engaged....you get the idea.)

There is a maturity of judgment and singularity of purpose in understanding that it's often better to allow someone else to take the first bungee jump, or wear the first midi-skirt, or ride the first mechanical bull. (The hackneyed inquiry, of course, is who had the courage to eat the first oyster?) There is plenty of time to get in the game afterwards, and the first entry rarely dominates: Just consider Osborne Computer, or Motorola cell phones, or Zenith televisions.

Your patience would have to be high with Bernie Madoff, and the Ponzi Scheme crews, but eventually you would have seen the early investors lose everything.[21] Early adapters, so revered, often get creamed.

Thriving personally isn't about being first, it's about being happy. This is a rough guess—I have zero empirical evidence—but you may relate to the belief that of all things one can own, time-shares represent the most grievously unhappy or uninvolved percentage of consumers. People make impulse decisions while on vacation and offered a pitiful assortment of junk and bad food to "take the tour," or they follow the inflated advice or others who want to talk themselves into having made a good investment that they've actually come to despise.

Now, you may have a terrific time-share arrangement (or you may be trying to salve your ego), but this is an example of an area where you're better off waiting, testing someone else's property, getting multiple

---

[21] The only place this doesn't hold true is in classic pyramid schemes, today euphemistically called "multi-level marketing," but no less corrupt, unethical, and reprehensible. When you make money only through bringing in new "members" and sell nothing in volume of discernable value, the numbers to sustain income for third and fourth generation investors soon swell to exponential zeros. In one of my earlier books, I calculated that by the 12th level of a pyramid scheme one would require the population of Cincinnati to repay investors at that stage.

stories, and generally biding your time. These things seem too good to be true, and they often are, because:

- It's much tougher to trade weeks elsewhere than the salespeople claim, so your choices are limited.

- You're confined to this vacation lifestyle, and often must pass up more interesting or varied possibilities.

- You're confined for a long period of time with very little chance of escaping from the contract or selling.

- The sheer vanilla of the surroundings and the neighbors becomes boring.

I have met a great many people who merely allow their weeks to lapse, give them to other family members, or trade them in for frequent flyer miles where allowed (that's what we came to do).

The DeLorean sports car was a horrible idea, and I'd recommend a "wait and see" game with the Tesla, the electric sports car, that can accelerate very fast, but is uncomfortable, lacks power steering, and has a mediocre 250-mile cruising range that, when exhausted, is not likely to be near the kind of recharging apparatus required to bring the beast back to life. (Do people really want a sports car that goes "whoosh"?) Low flush, environmentally-friendly toilets were quite popular and being installed frequently, until it was discovered that they required two or three flushes—using more water than a "normal" toilet—to accomplish what toilets were created to do.

It's generally a good idea not to be first or last, but somewhere within close proximity to the front. I remember when they conducted those infuriating, symbolic, random searches right at the airline gate. The search team had a quota, so they would always pull over the first person to board in first class (usually me) to make sure they began hitting their numbers, and they always nailed the last few people in coach to board because they were usually behind their quota. But the third person to board was virtually never searched. (This is based on painful personal trial and error.)

You needn't be the first to host the party, organize the trip, perform the intervention, try the host's molasses brulé, or study the lute. It's okay to ask around, observe, and merely participate. Yes, I know *someone* has to pick up the old baton, and *someone* has to take the initiative.

All I'm saying is that it needn't always be you. But if you insist, don't expect sympathy from me. The person in front tends to get the insects in the face.

They can hit you, they can knock you down, *and they can hurt you!*

Nothing drives me crazier than speakers spouting aphorisms amidst motivational mudslides. (Okay, Dr. Phil McGraw, the unlicensed hypocrite, drives me crazier, but I'm using hyperbole here.)

There is a guy in the National Speakers Association Professional Speaking Hall of Fame® with me, who is one of the very few remaining "motivational speakers."[22] He has an unhappy habit of actually proclaiming things such as, "They can hit you, but they can't knock you down."

What on earth does that mean? Of *course* they can knock you down. They can actually hurt you. Hell, they can knock you out and send you to intensive care.

Isn't the point not to be hit?

Arguing with insipid aphorisms is akin to playing tennis with an unstrung racket. But my point obtains: Empty-headed apothegms simply create empty efforts.

---

[22] Thank the gods. My position is that any speaker had better be motivational if he or she expects the audience to stay in the seats, but we had better have some solid content and not gelatinous pap.

One of the most bizarre documents to employ the English language that I've seen during the latter part of my lifetime is the Successories Catalog, which purports to provide positive sayings and invigorating mantras for self-improvement. "Only the lead dog ever sees a change of scenery!" would be representative, though I honestly don't know where that one came from—it might have been passed on by our Siberian Husky in the early 90s.[23]

We seem to be reliving the old Southern Baptist tent revivals, although at least those were intended to bring people closer to God. These days we seem intent on bringing people closer to an egalitarian mediocrity. Let me pose a few politically incorrect observations:

- We are not all good at all that we try. We should be judicious in that regard, and not be overly disappointed.

- One can be good at something and have low self-worth, or be poor at something and yet feel highly worthy. The point is to always have high self-worth while recognizing what you are good at and not so good at. (I can't dance, though can rock gently with a woman in my arms.)

- We all deserve an equal starting line and level playing field, but not an equal finish line. Talent, skill, and hard work should always "out."

- Society—the very one that you and I live within—is carried forward most efficaciously by promoting the best and the brightest, and not by giving everyone, regardless of talent, their "turn." (As legendary Kentucky basketball coach Adolph Rupp inquired, "If winning isn't important, why does anyone bother to keep score?")

---

[23] Inevitably, there are now anti-Successories accessories, which might proclaim, "Give it 110 percent effort when you don't have the talent to honestly compete and must claim something."

- Vapid bromides and mantras don't create better performance (or better English). They tend to provide pseudo-skills, enabling the low road passage: You don't have to try harder, you can simply kid yourself through emotionally manipulative phraseology.

If you choose to engage in positive self-talk or power language, that's a fine pursuit and there are honest-to-goodness scientists who have made a career of finding out how best to do so. To name just one, Google Martin Seligman and his books.

You can't Thrive tentatively. That is, you can't frame every statement as an interrogative. (Read this without conviction and end it with your voice increasing in pitch: "We should go on vacation." It will sound like, "Should we go on *vacation?*" This is called "uptalking," and women are more guilty of it than men, though quite a few men do it.) Nor do you Thrive by second-guessing yourself, and storing slogans in your cheeks like a chipmunk trodding hot coals.

Don't you love the speakers who ask you to raise your hand every nine seconds ("How many of you have had chicken-fried steak?") and consider that "audience participation"? Or the "trainers" who give you a workbook and ask you to fill in the blanks ("I need to _____ my teeth after every meal"[24]) as reinforcement? Or the person at the dinner party who responds to someone's admission that they have a crack habit, illegitimate child, attraction to their toaster, and dandruff with, "It's always darkest before the dawn," or "It's not what happens to you it's what you do about it!" (Yeah, okay, then at least tell me what I should specifically do about the toaster fetish.)

If you want someone to follow you, find out what's in *their* self-interest and then exemplify the behavior that you expect them to emulate. If you want to carve out a new route for yourself, examine your own best self-interest and find someone who exemplifies it so that they can be your avatar.

---

[24] The acceptable entry is "remove."

DIGRESSION

I worked for a major hospital's CEO on a number of projects. On every available wall of the facility was a plaque with "Our Basic Values," and the fourth value down of eight was, "We respect our people." (It's always the fourth one down, these are preprinted somewhere in Latvia.)

Right in front of this ubiquitous propaganda you could see hospital managers ruthlessly beating up people, emotionally and professionally.

The CEO—I am not making this up—said to me one day, "I can't understand the morale problem we have here. We proclaim our beliefs in public all over the place."

"Bill," I asked gently, "do you think people believe what they read on the walls or what they see in the halls?"

If your example is an empty-headed motivational speaker, you are likely to become one yourself. If your model is a pragmatic, high-content speaker, then you will be prone to walk (and talk) in that direction.

As mentioned earlier, for every motto and saying there is an equal and opposite motto and saying ("Haste makes waste," "Get there firstest with the mostest."). Call it Alan's Fifth Law of Mantradynamics. Adages and apothegms have a calming effect because they attempt to alleviate our necessity to think, to apply discipline, and to take accountability. They are verbal placebos and you no more Thrive after them than you would lose the flu after a medical placebo. (Yes, you don't have to convince me that psychology and beliefs play a strong role in behavior, ergo my recommendation of positive self-talk. But give your id some credit.)

If you listen to the great stories, songs, and even poetry, you'll find tremendous creativity and innovation. The substance seldom mindlessly repeats. Instead, the present builds upon the past in urging us to action.

> " She gets too hungry for dinner at eight,
>
> She loves the theater, but never comes late;
>
> She'd never bother with people she'd hate,
>
> That's why the lady is a tramp."[25]

It just sort of beats the hell out of something like, "She's her own person and they can't make her anyone else."

They *can* knock you down and knock you out, especially if you're distracted by loony sayings that make no sense and belong in fortune cookies.

I've been thrown out of better rooms than this…. just earlier today

Excuse me, but what's the worst thing that can happen to you in anyone's office? I realize that on soaps and some series, people are defenestrated, seduced, and/or threatened.

But that's not the real world.

Stop worrying about what's going to happen to you when you walk through the real or metaphorical door. The one thing I will guarantee—really, I'll give you 1000-to-1—is that you're going to be walking out again. (If you're carried in, all bets are off.) So the focus needs to be on what transpires between your entrance and exit.

---

[25] By Lorenz Hart and Richard Rodgers for "Babes in Arms," 1937.

Here are some hints for handling strange environments and unfamiliar surroundings:

- **Take a few moments to take it in**. Look around: Don't leap into the middle of a conversation as if it's a rugby scrum. (One of my favored techniques is to stick my head in ahead of time. Sometimes the secretary will offer you a seat in the other person's office to wait, or sometimes the empty office door is open, and I take a look. I want to familiarize myself with what is otherwise unfamiliar.[26])

- **Think about meeting on neutral ground**. Conference rooms are usually sufficiently universal and banal so that you don't have any surprises. Or meet in a restaurant, particularly one that you know. Or invite the other person to your club. (This last alternative is somewhat difficult if you don't *have* a club.)

- **After you absorb the environment, focus on the other person**. Don't miss early body language or statements. If you ignore the foundation, the barn is going to collapse.

- **Set the agenda**. Simply state, "I know your time is tight, as is mine. I have three issues I'd like to discuss and I imagine you have a few. Why don't we list them, set some priorities, and then invest our time accordingly?" That immediately establishes you as a peer (*our time is tight*), and allows you to actually create the music to dance to.

- **Search for patterns indicating behavior**. In other words, is the office carefully organized or cluttered? Does the other person allow for interruptions or turn others away? Are you offered refreshments or not? Do you face each other across a desk or do you sit on comfortable couches? Does the other person ask about you and your background, or dive into the business at hand immediately?

---

[26] This is an old professional speaking trick, wherein you walk on stage in a deserted room prior to the event, so that you can get the "feel" of the place.

- Is there anything you recognize that will further the relationship: a photo, a memento, an award, a piece of art, the view, the furniture?

We are all at a bit of a disadvantage on someone else's turf, but that needn't be permanent or fatal. After a while, the unfamiliar becomes the familiar (and after a while, you realize there's nothing you haven't seen and experienced before).

I always think back to actual places I've been tossed out of: the original Le Cirque restaurant, because I didn't have a tie, even though there was a guy without a jacket or tie seated not far behind the super-arrogant *maître d'*, who is long gone, bless his black heart; the inside of a cross-channel steamer, because my friends and I could only afford the cheapest tickets and the crew made it a point of honor to keep us out on the cold decks in the dark of night heading from England to France; Kensington Park in London because a delightful young woman and I had not noticed that night had fallen and the park was closed; a private club in Summit, New Jersey, because my wife's and my background was not sufficiently consistent with the existing members (and to be more accurate, they actually never even allowed us in); and a high-rollers room in a Vegas Casino where I had moseyed up to a table, placed a $25 bet, and was shown a sign (and subsequently, the door) that said, "$2500 minimum bet."

We all get thrown out of places, most of which we shouldn't really want to be in. But you can limit the chances of this by understanding the environment, seeking out associational clues, and acting like you belong there.

The care and feeding of the bruised ego

In coaching, counseling, and mentoring thousands of people globally, I've encountered few factors which cause more angst, fear, and vacillation than fretful egos.

I'm not talking about the giant ego that devours all in its path like the zipped-up Japanese monsters crushing Tokyo with regularity in the horror films of the 50s. At least these are easily identifiable, you can run from them, and sooner or later someone discovers the death ray or sonic boom that dissolves them into the likes of whining, splattered puddles of nontoxic goo.

Rather, I'm referring to the stately, modest, quite proper egos which are threatened by someone pointing out they are using the wrong fork to eat the soup.

"Alan, we're seeking success, not perfection," said one of my therapists 15 years or more ago (for $110 an hour[27]). The readily bruised ego rules the psychic playing field under these condition:

1. You crave perfection to avoid being critiqued in any way.

2. You take critique as personal rejection and/or attacks on your self-worth.

Admit it: Have you been forced to breathe the exhaust of this toxic tandem?

The irony of people not budging or refusing to disclose or avoiding all risk because of a metaphorical bruise which will occur completely unseen to others and cause no physical impairment is astounding, but devastating. There is an underlying lack of self-worth which peels the layers off the ego and leaves it, like a shucked clam, vulnerable to all sorts of unpleasant contingencies, such as voracious sea gulls.

---

[27] Which is why I never give any service provider or vender any of my books and generally suggest that they're really not relevant.

A woman was a guest speaker at an event for which I was the emcee. In an obviously memorized and scripted speech, she made a couple of errors that a professional would catch but an audience probably wouldn't. She ended 10 minutes early, not a cardinal sin, and was escorted off stage by me with very nice applause from the audience.

Backstage, she said to me, "How was it?"

I said, "Fine." And she burst into tears. I've driven quite a few people to real and symbolic tears, but never with merely "fine."

"What's wrong?" I shouted above the sobbing.

" 'Fine' isn't good enough," she wailed. "I have to be great."

Now, isn't that a nice burden to walk around with?

Here is an example of the difference and relationship between efficacy—competency to achieve results—and self-worth—how you value yourself. We commented earlier that you can be good at something but not feel you deserve it, or you can feel good about yourself but not feel that your talents are being sufficiently applied and acknowledged.

Albert Bandura (sort of the "rock star" of behavioral psychology in some circles) highlights the fact that one's abilities and one's belief in self are independent variables. I would add to this that people who have high efficacy but low self-worth feelings fit the "imposter" definition, whereby they don't feel they deserve to be where they are and hence some day will be "found out" or "outed." They feel lucky to "get away" with their current status for the time being (which often lasts 25 years!).

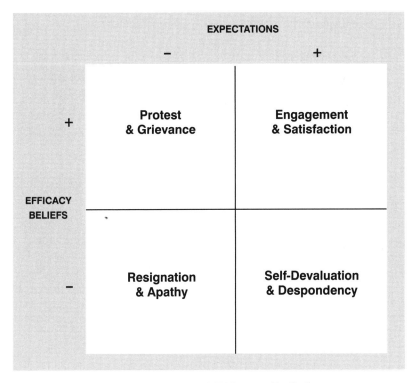

Expectations and Efficacy Beliefs[28]

We need to tuck our egos away, because when they are so exposed and perched on the surface they are vulnerable to every shrug and moan from passing pedestrians. We also need to bury our egos in deep bunkers, so that we know they are safe and even a direct hit isn't going to cause any damage.

[28] This chart is from his Albert Bandura's book *Self-Efficacy* (Macmillan, 1997).

How do we do this?

- **Act like the mafia**. It's never personal, it's only about business. An Australian or a New Yorker will both tell you (with equally strange accents) that you're wrong, misguided, and foolish, and then offer to buy you a beer. Don't take it personally, and remember, it's up to you to determine if they're right or if they've already had too much to drink.

- **Treat questions and objections as signs of interest**. The worst and most dangerous people are those who are apathetic, since they offer no sign of acceptance or rejection and you never know how they feel. But people who object or merely question are *exhibiting signs of interest*. Don't treat them like plague carriers.

- **Separate the factual from the *ad hominem***. If someone is using observed behavior and evidence, then listen, e.g., "You never established eye contact," or "There are typos in the slides," or "You have celery protruding from your incisors." However, ignore and even rebut the judgmental, e.g., "You are not a team player," or "Clothing selection is beyond your abilities," or "You're arrogant." (I'm always spending time ignoring this last one. Seriously, it's the rebuttal of people who don't know how to argue with you on an intellectual basis, so they resort to psychological warfare.) Don't bother with judgmental accusations, but do get the celery out of your teeth.

- **Look at the *gestalt* and never generalize from a specific**. One instance, one example, one situation does not symbolize or encapsulate your worth. View your life, your history, your probable future. A single victory or a single defeat does not define you (and those who allow either to do so often become clinically depressed, and is the danger of trodding over hot coals). View your entire presence and you're much more unlikely to allow a single episode to damage your self-worth.

A strong, resilient, and protected ego is at the heart of Thriving. It is a Golconda that is constantly renewing and rewarding.

Churchillian logic: It's courage that counts

Perhaps the best source of British quotes since Oscar Wilde,[29] Winston Churchill observed that "success is never final and failure seldom fatal—it's courage that counts."

Ironically, you need just a modicum of courage to succeed these days. In most cases, simply holding your ground will put you ahead of the pack, since the pack retreats, like sandpipers before the incoming tide, at the merest hint of turbulence.

The Aztec warriors were renowned for tethering their ankles to a stake in the ground (hence, the bromide today, to put a stake in the ground) and fighting on that spot without the possibility of retreat. That sounds heroic and mighty, except they couldn't *advance* either, at least not very easily.

Overcoming the fear of failure means being willing to fail. The best race car drivers have been in collisions, the best golfers have hit the ball in the water, the best actors have gone up on their lines, and the best entrepreneurs have been broke. If you allow setbacks to become terminal failures, then you have no hope, no recourse, no tomorrow.

Resilient people do not regard failure as a personal statement about either their worth or their efficacy. And herein is the secret:

If your learning philosophy is internally focused, you will act as if you have learned everything necessary to succeed. However, when the inevitable setback slams you, you will have nothing left. You will have shot your bolt (to use another ancient, military bromide), there is nothing left. After all, if you know all you need to know, and it wasn't enough, what else is there?

---

[29] A note on the dumbing-down of our times: In a prior book, I cited Oscar Wilde's quotes twice. The permissions editor told me that she would not allow the book to go into production until I had signed permission from Oscar Wilde to use his quotes. You cannot make this stuff up.

People who consciously or subconsciously regard their learning as internally focused become depressed easily, do not bounce back from setback, and show little resilience. They are often easily thrown and don't recover. Once off the horse, even though otherwise able to ride again, they choose not to remount.

If your learning philosophy is externally focused, you will act as though you need to access other sources to continue to succeed. When the inevitable setback undermines you, you will seek out the additional learning and skills to overcome it and prevent it next time. If there is all that learning out there, then there is no limit to what you can integrate and apply in any conditions.

People who regard their learning as externally focused are resilient, never take setbacks personally, don't generalize from negative specifics, and resemble the Weeble that wobbles but doesn't fall down. Once off the horse, they bounce up and get back on, sometimes so quickly that the horse hasn't even had a chance to slow up.

Instead of empty phrases we all need clear beliefs and pragmatic skills to Thrive. Telling yourself that they can't knock you down is inherently false, since we all get knocked down, sooner or later. But believing that setbacks are learning experiences and not commentaries on our worth, and searching out and applying new skills to overcome the deficiency or the challenge, are what create healthy and prosperous adults (and, for that matter, children and teens).

We fear things and situations that can't really hurt us: public speaking, crowds, heights, social conversation, powerful people in our presence, entertaining, shopping, writing, and so on. I've met people and counseled people with all these "afflictions" and more. The fear is irrational because it not based on observable behavior or evidence. As just one example, about 95 percent[30] of all people attending a speech or training

---

[30] The other five percent are distracted by personal issues (spouse spat, traffic jam, money problems) or have behavioral disorders which relish in *schadenfreude*.

program of any kind want it to succeed. The speaker has the support of the audience, not its antipathy, enmity, or skepticism. No healthy human wants to go home and say, "What a great day, I wasted two hours of my time while I watched a speaker go down in flames. It was totally useless."

The fear isn't of the actual, it's of the invented. (So are some of the remedies—imagining the audience is naked is one of the dumbest, most moronic techniques I can think of, and, of course, one of the most recommended!) We owe ourselves the personal dignity of overcoming fantasy causes and fantasy cures (such as trodding over hot coals and thinking it proves anything other than the power of perspiration of the feet, not exactly a key job aid). That's the kind of courage I'm talking about in order to Thrive: What do I need to do to overcome my basically unfounded and silly fears?

Being afraid of the dark as a child is no different from being afraid of mice or public speaking as an adult. The fear is a vast overreaction to the contextual situation, although at least you can excuse the child who has integrated far less learning than the adult. Superstitions are merely attempts to organize fears without having to understand them—it's easier to remember not to put your hat on a table or open an umbrella indoors than to deal with whatever causes such hysteria.

It's courage that counts. The courage to face fears logically and rationally, using formal or informal help if you need it. It's the courage to understand the power of an external locus of learning. And it's the courage to say, "I'm not here to merely get by and survive. I'm here to Thrive."

We're not here to stick our toe in the water. We're here to make waves.

CHAPTER 5

Why fish don't wish: The four-second attention span

You won't get attention unless you pay attention

This is an age of "instant air time." Anyone who wants to shoot the breeze, cite an inanity, or engage in any kind of bloviation has the means to do it instantly on Twitter, Linkedin, Facebook, or dozens of other platforms. I especially adore people who want to link with me "because they trust me so much." The problem is that I've never heard of them and it's an automated invitation, but, hell, it's a nice sentiment, right?

We're besieged by more "noise" than ever before, and in our infantile rants to try to gain attention above and beyond the cacophony, no one is listening. No one, truth be told, is paying much attention. Social media, the propaganda assures, are excellent for "amplification." And that is exactly the problem.

If you can't recall it, forget it

Goodman Ace is hardly a household name these days, but at one time he was a reigning master of TV quiz shows, not the pseudo-intellectual froth of *Jeopardy* or the pathetic voyeurism of reality shows, but rather the mindless banality of *To Tell the Truth* or *Let's Make A Deal*. That's his citation leading this segment: "If you can't recall it, forget it."

That's always struck me as the pinnacle of shallow existence. Don't worry about anything except what's in your mind at this very moment, which for many human beings is generally about eating, sex, or a bodily function, usually in that order.

When I was studying for my doctorate in psychology[31] I took as many peripheral courses as I could get credit for, since the subject was starting to drive me crazy, pun intended. I wound up reading a lot about animals and found in one ancient and tangential work, that fish have a four-second attention span.

If that's true, it's small wonder that fisherman can show up everyday in the same place and catch the same fish. Because the stupid-ass trout is swimming along saying, "Nice water today, hey, there's something that pathetically is trying to look like a worm, it's obviously fake, but I think I'll bite it." Next thing you know, he's hooked with some degree of pain and released. He hits the water and a few seconds later is saying, "Nice water today, hey....."

I think a lot of people are the same way. They are incapable of paying attention, and this was Goodman Ace's great discovery for his successful TV shows. You didn't have to remember anything, just react in the moment. If you can't recall it, it's not important.

Now, lest you think I make light of this or made up my research, I direct you to an outstanding book by Margaret Wheatley called, *Leadership and the New Science* (Berrett-Koehler, 2006). Therein, Ms. Wheatley posits that consciousness is a factor of processing information, and that, therefore, a dog has a higher degree of consciousness than a snail, because dogs are capable of processing much more information than snails.

---

[31] I have a non-traditional PhD, which I readily admit but make no excuses about. I suffered through 2.5 years of class work, research involving Merck, Hewlett-Packard, and Marine Midland Bank (now HSBC), a year on a suicide hotline, two years on the board of a shelter for battered woman, one rejected dissertation, one accepted dissertation, and an oral defense in front of professors from Harvard and USC. So there you have it in case anyone wants to throw stones, as a defense lawyer attempted during discovery when I was an expert witness. She had two dozen of my books and hundreds of my articles on the table in front of her, but could only focus on the fact that my school wasn't in the right accreditation column.

I began to think about that and realized that people process information in vastly different ways and with subtly different devices. Consequently, *some people have a higher consciousness than others.*

You heard that here, that's my story, and I'm sticking to it.

You don't believe me? Then consider this:

- The person who stops immediately in front of a descending escalator, oblivious to the pileup about to commence behind.

- The individual who chats up the bank teller about her grandchildren or his new car while the line for withdrawals snakes its way out into the parking lot.

- The person who consistently walks into the wrong rest room, despite the clear markings (I'm not talking about those who do this deliberately; that's another book).

- The driver who moseys over into the next lane in front of an 18-wheeler, not on the phone, not on the radio, just not on this planet.

I could go on, and so could you, but some of you have lost track, so snap out of it!

We're all so busy talking, posting, tweeting, texting, recording, linking, inviting, and generally showing off, that we're not listening, not learning, and not growing. We're surviving in the din, not Thriving above the clamor.

In all candor, are you able to:

- Quickly recall and find things, so that you have "just in time knowledge," when you need it, where you need it?

- Put together salient facts to create meaningful, useful information "on the fly" with friends, clients, and colleagues?

- Create new intellectual capital regularly by recombining disparate elements of ideas and approaches which you encounter?

- Readily recall experiences, lessons learned, causes for victories and defeats, so that you rarely repeat errors and usually replicate successes?

- Process more information than your dog or your snail? (Are you walking him, or is he walking you?)

If you want to Thrive, you *must* rise above what will become an ever-increasing noise level. And you don't do that by shouting louder, you do it by *listening* more selectively and more carefully.

Stampeding stimuli—making sense out of chaos

How do you make rational sense out of the chaos around us? There are, at this writing, approximately 200 million blogs globally on the Internet. That's a blog for almost every adult citizen in the U.S., for example. And 95 percent of them comprise mindless crap, stream-of-consciousness banality, hucksterism, obscenity, and just plain poor writing. (Many, done with primitive software templates, don't even identify the author.)

There is one guy I found in Australia who merely copies small business guru David Maister's blog postings verbatim, and claims them as his own. (Thus, if Maister talks about his latest book, this guy talks about it as if he wrote it!) I wrote to ask him just how he had the audacity to do this, and he never responded, of course. I'm assuming his audience is composed of the odd monotreme and dingo, but you never know.[32]

Here is how you Thrive despite the chaos around you.

---

[32] There is a website that allows you to input any one of your online pages and check to see if anyone else is using it on their site: www.copyscape.com/.

Alan's Tips for Making Sense of the Riot Around Us

- **Limit your time on social sites**. Treat them as a hobby and, as any hobby, you get to them in your spare time. If you're posting on Facebook even once an hour, or trying to gain contacts on Linkedin every day, or following two dozen people on Twitter, it's the equivalent of spending six hours a day collecting stamps, or spending all day tuning the car's engine, or not coming out of the garden for the entire weekend.

  You know who engages in that kind of behavior? *Retired* people, people with WAY too much time on their hands, that's who.

- **Stop slavishly listening to series and periodical offerings**. If you were to take a look at TED, for example (www.ted.com), you'll find some of the most provocative and original thinking anywhere, and something ideally suited to the web. But you'll also find some things of no interest to you or, occasionally, poorly done or executed.

  There's no need to watch everything, you must apply discrimination. You don't read the entire newspaper (those of you still living in cities that have them), you scan the headlines for items of interest, I would think. The same holds true for all media. There is no law against fast-forwarding a podcast, download, DVD, or anything else to see if it gets any better. Life is too short merely to hope for the best as the speaker drones on about "being your own best friend."

- **Reconcile with whom you agree and disagree to *calibrate what you hear and read***. This sounds strange, but it's very powerful. An example: There are some book and theater critics with whom I do not agree philosophically. If they pan a book or theatrical release for certain reasons I may be just as prone to pursue it as I am from a critic with whom I generally agree who endorses it.

If you do this consistently, you'll quickly make decisions about what makes sense to invest time in and what is probably the La Brea Tar Pit of time investment. In my experience, when the reviewers in *The Wall Street Journal* (whom I respect) and the reviewers in *The Providence Journal* disagree antipodally, I know I've got solid evidence.

- **Never allow a non-human, and certainly not a non-oxygen breathing entity, to interrupt you**. I suppose the dogs have a way of gaining attention, for example, threatening to vomit on your outgoing mail, but allowing a computer to interrupt you with email alerts, meeting reminders, RSS fees, and flossing guidelines is just insane.

  There is enough human noise out there that is aided and abetted by other living creatures (I would approve your immediately ceasing typing an article should a tarantula suddenly scuttle onto the keyboard, for example). But to allow mindless mechanisms to further add to our attention deficit is nutso.

- **Remember that time is not about resource but about priority**. We all have 24 hours in the day. That doesn't change, thanks to leap year. Consequently, there is no issue about creating more of it. You can make another dollar, but not another minute. So that leaves us solely with how we use it.

  Therefore, everything becomes a function of the priorities we create. If everything is a priority, nothing is a priority. We must create triage among the issues in our lives. If you tell me that you wish you could see your kid's dance recital or soccer game, but just don't have the time, you're really telling me that you just have more important things to do—higher priority demands on that time.

- **Break projects and goals into manageable chunks**. Everyone finds it easy to say, "I want to write a book," or "I must look at new homes." But they find it extraordinarily difficult to say, "I'm going to write half of chapter one tomorrow at 10 am," or "I'm going to spend Wednesday between 2 and 5 working with a real estate agent on the East Side."

There is no such thing as a "long term project," since all projects must start now if they are to reach fruition and conclusion. That's why so many people get lost amidst the noise—they have no nearby handhold with which to extricate themselves. A "book" is a distant island; but "half a chapter tomorrow" is an easy swim.

- **Separate avocation from occupation**. An occupation is usually a career (not merely a "job") that one engages in to create sufficient monetary income to support one's personal goals and preferences. This may include advancement, enhanced expertise, even fame, but certainly disciplined application with payment received commensurate with value, as a fair test.

  An avocation is a pastime, a delight, a bagatelle, which entertains and amuses, even engrosses, but is not measured in monetary reward or in advancement.[33] It is generally measured in terms of satisfaction and comfort for the individual (playing a guitar) or others around the individual (listening to the guitar player). To confuse these two is to neither prosper nor delight. You wind up working for free and relaxing through work, not exactly part of the playbook.

- **Become an object of interest so that people seek you out**. In this manner, you needn't compete for "air time" or report on each bar of soap you've used in the shower on Twitter. Your Facebook page needn't have photos of your lint collection. You need to be sought, not to seek.

---

[33] Okay, so there are exceptions, like a 12th degree black belt, and Eagle Scout, and a grandmaster chess champion, but you get my drift.

As opposed to rising above the masses, this technique inspires the masses to part for you. True objects of interest don't have to tout their activities or their accomplishments. That's what paparazzi are for.

In one of my programs, "Moving from Six Figures to Seven," which we call 627, I ask participants to keep a two-month journal of time use prior to the program. What we've inevitably found is that there is a surfeit of time available for professional and personal pursuits. But there are two major inhibitors:

1. The time is not wisely used or even controlled. It is subject to others' interference (family, friends, "obligations") and to environmental interference (email urges, phone calls, distractions).

2. The priorities are not intelligently set, are missing, or are even set by others. Consequently, what is a surfeit of time is usurped.

I remember a time management specialist by the name of Bill Oncken who delivered a half-crazed, shouted workshop as part of his shtick. But one thing he said always stayed with me: Never let them leave the monkey on your desk.

What he meant is that no one should come into your office and leave you with more than you had before they entered, and leave with less than they had after they entered. I have extrapolated that philosophy successfully to life itself: Don't send me your newsletters, email alerts, meeting reminders, blog postings, unsolicited feedback, junk mail, or anything else *unless I specifically request it.*

Am I totally successful in avoiding this social space debris? No, but I'd bet I'm far more successful than you, and far more in control of the priority setting in my life. YOU are not using MY time, unless I permit it because it makes sense for me, too, win/win. If I don't do this for myself, who will?

If you don't do it for yourself, who will? And over the course of years of not doing it, how much of your precious, non-renewable time will you surrender to the noise and chaos around you?

Stimuli will increase exponentially. There will be holographic images before you know it (there are already virtual meetings with full screens in the room from remote locations[34]). You will have one phone number that follows you everywhere. Movies, theater, TV, online videos are now largely available on demand on your iPhone or PDA. You'll be playing interactive games with someone in China while waiting in the dentist's office.

All of that will increase, and so will the demands for "air time," and so will the resultant noise and chaos. You've got to make sense of it for your own life, or you'll drown in the medial mire.

Would salmon still swim upstream if they owned choppers?

I was watching one of these "funniest video" shows, and there was a clip of a guy catching a salmon with a rod and reel. As he pulls it in, a very large grizzly bear appears on the run out of the woods, grabs the fish off the hook in shallow water and begins to trot away.

The fisherman throws his rod at the bear, then begins to chase the bear to try to get the fish back! The bear, apparently astounded, runs back into the woods with the fish. I don't know what happened after that, but I do know the salmon was dead.

Would these fish keep swimming upstream, against nature, trapped by intelligent (the bear) predators, and really dumb (the fisherman) hunters who know their path if they didn't have to?

I think not.

---

[34] We had a private kitchen tour after dinner of the magnificent Per Se Restaurant in New York, and chef Thomas Keller has a huge screen on the kitchen wall of his French Laundry Restaurant in California, where they, reciprocally could see us.

Yet why do so many people pursue paths that take them in harm's way repeatedly, against all odds, and with great stress and pain? I present to you "The Calf Path," read by the provost of Rutgers University during one of our pre-graduation activities. I asked his secretary to send me a copy.[35]

The Calf Path
by Sam Walter Foss (1858-1911)

One day, through the primeval wood,
A calf walked home, as good calves should;
But made a trail all bent askew,
A crooked trail, as calves all do.
Since then three hundred years have fled,
And, I infer, the calf is dead.
But still he left behind his trail,
And thereby hangs my moral tale.

The trail was taken up next day
By a lone dog that passed that way;
And then a wise bellwether sheep
Pursued the trail o'er vale and steep,
And drew the flock behind him, too,
As good bellwethers always do.
And from that day, o'er hill and glade,
Through those old woods a path was made.

And many men wound in and out,
And dodged and turned and bent about,
And uttered words of righteous wrath
Because 'twas such a crooked path;
But still they followed—do not laugh—
The first migrations of that calf.

---

[35] Of course in this day and age you can Google it and find 12 different variations, which makes my copy on the provost's stationery from 42 years ago all that much more precious.

This forest path became a lane,
That bent, and turned, and turned again.
This crooked lane became a road,
Where many a poor horse with his load
Toiled on beneath the burning sun,
And traveled some three miles in one.
And thus a century and a half
They trod the footsteps of that calf.

The years passed on in swiftness fleet.
The road became a village street,
And this, before men were aware,
A city's crowded thoroughfare,
And soon the central street was this
Of a renowned metropolis;
And men two centuries and a half
Trod in the footsteps of that calf.
A hundred thousand men were led
By one calf near three centuries dead.

For men are prone to go it blind
Along the calf-path of the mind,
And work away from sun to sun
To do what other men have done.
They follow in the beaten track,
And out and in, and forth and back,
And still their devious course pursue,
To keep the path that others do.

They keep the path a sacred groove,
Along which all their lives they move;
But how the wise old wood-gods laugh,
Who saw the first primeval calf!

Every day many of us put ourselves in a position of risk, or stress, or pain, or non-clinical depression, or discomfort because we believe there is only one way to reach the spawning ground, one path to follow. Despite being sentient creatures, we pursue some primeval urge to duplicate and replicate, but not initiate.[36]

And so I call on you to ask yourself these questions, in candor and brutal honesty:

- Do you maintain relationships that are damaging to you?

- Do you continue to work at a job that doesn't reward you sufficiently?

- Do you expose yourself to harsh, unsolicited feedback regularly?

- Do you refuse opportunities because you feel you don't deserve them?

- Do you usually defer to the wishes of others, even in contradiction of your own, best interests?

- Do you constantly wish you were in another place, doing another thing?

- Do you continually daydream about "What if?"

- Do you have entire days with few or no redeeming features or rewards?

- Do you feel helpless to create or accept changes to your life?

- Do you have little variety in your life from day to day?

---

[36] The perhaps apocryphal, popular story, is that our modern, high speed trains have the track gauge that they do (width between rails) as a result of the ancient Roman trails forged in Britain by the chariot wheels of the soldiers. The wheels were aligned so as to meet the breadth of the shoulders of the two horses providing the power. No one ever bothered, presumably, to investigate a better or more efficient width.

If you answered "yes" to *any of these*, you are swimming upstream amidst the predators. You are following the calf path. The more "yeses," the more you are trapped and mired.

You need to change this in order to Thrive, and you need to sustain and perpetuate yourself if you answered "no" to all of them in order to continue to Thrive.

Fortunately, you have the means to do so.

Occam's Razor: A close shave is a good thing

Sir William of Occam, a 14th Century British philosopher (what we'd call today in pedestrian prose a "thought leader," ugh) posited that the easiest route is usually the best, and hence "Occam's Razor" became a metaphor.

The man knew whereof he spoke.

I have always looked at destinations—business, vacation, personal, civic, hobbies, you name it—and have worked backwards attempting to find the easiest and quickest solution. This was, at first, simply intuitive, until I realized after six years of dealing with strategy in corporations and seven years of dealing with therapists in anxiety, that my driving force is laziness. And that's nothing to shake a stick at, assuming you had the energy and volition to find a stick and shake it.

People and organizations (and teams and committees and task forces and colonies of amoeba) do not Thrive when they focus on the present and tentatively seek out the alternative for moving forward. I remind you: We are not here to stick our toes in the water.

We are here to make waves.

The worst thing for the military and for you and me is to fail to keep the objective as our priority and to instead become mired in the routes to get there. Another "thought leader," the philosopher George Santayana, described a fanatic as "someone who loses site of his goals and consequently redoubles his efforts." I don't know about you, but I've had my share of fanatics surrounding me in corporate environments.

When we're merely considering alternatives, and we have a limited attention span to begin with, we hop around like people doing those nutty Tony Robbins fire walks whose feet *don't* perspire. I don't care how positive your attitude, hot coals and hot ideas, unbounded by a goal and unprotected by insulation, can make you hop like a rabid kangaroo.

No one will admire you for taking a long time to do anything. I remember in Rome seeing Hadrian's Villa, and the tour guide explaining it took 400 years to complete. My immediate shock was that, somehow, Hadrian and I had been using the same general contractor on our building improvements. I'm not impressed by length, I'm impressed by quality. Solve 90 percent of my problems in 10 days and I'm much more grateful than your solving 100 percent of my problems in a year (by which time I undoubtedly have new problems).

Speed isn't of the essence. Speed is the essence. In a cyberspace world of instant communication, time shifting, and immediate gratification, the shortest route is always going to be the best route if you simply apply yourself.

The problem, of course, is that a multiplicity of choices, which accompanies the Internet world, confounds the process and keeps enticing you off the direct path.

In high school, I lettered in the sprints in my freshman year because they were over in about 10 seconds and 20 seconds respectively[37] I didn't have to think. I met a fighter pilot once, who had gone on to be a major general, and he growled repeatedly about bomber command: "Who wants to fly a plane by committee?" In the longer distance races, I found

---

[37] Way back then, we ran the 100-yard and 220-yard dashes, pre-metric.

runners constantly psyching themselves out by considering when to pass, when to hang back, how to avoid being boxed in, and so on.

In my sprints, the gun went off and then I was either congratulating the winner or being congratulated. The gun scares you to death and then you run for your life.

Simple.

That's not a bad formula for life. Skip the next paragraph if you are not anal-retentive, read carefully if you are:

That's not to say that you should be precipitous in all actions, or bet the family farm on a whim, or charge into a career because an astrologer or fortune cookie advised it. You want to pay due diligence to your kid's schooling and your investments. And the person you marry may merit something more than perfunctory consideration. Resume normal programming below.

I've actually made some great "sprint-like" decisions which have served me well, and if I had taken another three weeks to try to make a "better" one, the improvements would have been dysfunctional, a terribly negative ROI.

If you want to Thrive, get there fast, however imperfectly. The surfeit of choices these days actually freezes people. They can't choose a flat screen TV, let alone an investment plan or career. The search for "perfection" vitiates the ability to achieve happiness. If you're constantly worried or anxious because you have an aisle seat instead of a window (or vice versa) in first class, or you have a four-top table and not a banquette in the excellent restaurant, or you have a 5.6 percent return instead of a neighbor's 5.9 percent return in a tough economy, you simply don't deserve to be happy because you've failed to appreciate good fortune.

You're searching for perfection and not success.

One of the most essential keys to Thriving *is to accept imperfect success.* I would rather watch the Patriots win the Super Bowl with a few losses, than lose after a perfect season. (And so would they.) I would rather lose a few battles in order to win the war. I don't mind it if six people out of a hundred don't like my speech if the rest do, and I don't mind if all hundred don't like it so long as the buyer does!

General Nathan Bedford Forrest, the famed Confederate cavalry raider, remarked that his success was based on "getting there firstest with the mostest." (There is evidence that the good general was well educated and actually noted that he tried to move the greatest force to the battle in the shortest time, but that, as they say, is not as good of a sound bite.) You don't have to get there first with everyone, nor do you even have to get there first.

For many years, as I've noted, Hewlett-Packard was famous for being the second company into a given market, having learned from the mistakes of the first. Steve Jobs admitted that his success at Apple, one of the iconic innovative leaders of our time, was that he tried to "jump on the next big thing." I'm an Apple advocate, but not one product they produce that I've tried is perfect. But they're awfully good, and almost always ahead of the pack. And the second version is always better than the first, the third better than the second.

Ask yourself, catholically, what is the quickest means to your ends? Do you need the best television or just one of the myriad really good ones? Do you need an hour meeting, or just some face-to-face time?[38] Do you really need a music system that only dogs can appreciate? (I find this one of the all-time most ludicrous violations of Occam's Razor. People can no more tell one good music system from another than they can tell "free range" chicken from well-prepared road kill in a restaurant, except for the price.)

So go back four centuries and consider Sir William's insightful dictum. What is the shortest route, the easiest route, to your desired ends? It

---

[38] I consistently reject requests for "an hour of my time." How the hell do you know you need an hour? And if I agree to it, it's a sure bet that you'll find a way to fill it up.

may not be perfect, but will it get you there with ease, fulfillment, and confidence?

Or are you too busy taking all the side trips to the flea markets and bazaars where the prices are not even as good as the shops downtown, but they know a tourist when they see one?

Life is short only because we're not paying attention

Near the end of Arthur Miller's masterpiece, "Death of a Salesman," Willy Loman's wife yells about her husband's passing, "Attention must be paid!" Isolated, it's a banal line, trite and insipid, an empty plea. But in context, it's a seminal moment in an iconic play.

We seldom view our lives in context and, thus, fail to pay the attention it (and we) deserve. We're fond of saying "life is short" in order to justify yet another plasma television or a trip to Nepal using credit. Human life is short compared to a parrot or land tortoise, perhaps, but a mayfly lives for 24 hours on a good day and we all know that dogs' life spans are far too short (an oversight by God that I'm confident one evolutionary day He will correct).

Gender and ethnicity aside, humans with decent access to preventive and contingent health care measures in peaceful societies live to 75 or 80 years of age, and most of it is high quality these days. One's lifestyle may have to change given certain inevitabilities of aging, but a combination of better health, more options for the "elderly," and the demands of erratic economies on savings has created a longer-lived, longer-working, longer-viewing populace. (Playwright Tom Stoppard had the greatest line I've ever read about this: "Age is such a high price to pay for maturity.")

When our attention span is brief, our life experiences tend to be brief. We think life is short because we're looking backward in nostalgia or forward in anticipation.

We should be looking around in awareness.

Instead, like racehorses or plow horses—that is, despite our current pace—we wear the blinders that keep us looking in one direction and aren't willing or able to look around in comprehension of the condition of our lives. Life seems short because we're not appreciating the great existence we live at the moment, even though we pretend to capture it. (My uncle asked at one family gathering, "What happens to all these pictures you all take? I never see them again. Do you look at them? Are they displayed in the rooms of your homes? Do you take them out periodically? Actually, they usually reside on a CD, or in a file, or on iPhoto, gathering cyberdust.)

What can we do to enjoy the present more than four seconds or so at a time? Here are my suggestions for "living in the moment."

Alan's Live-in-the-Moment Criteria

- **Stop rushing in and out**. Have a drink before your meal and linger over coffee or an after-dinner drink later. Talk to the wait staff and management. If you're going to a play, have dinner in a restaurant nearby. If you're leaving in the seventh inning of the ball game, or prior to the play's curtain call, or prior to the priest in the recessional, you're simply cheating yourself in order to avoid some meaningless traffic.

- **Comprehend why you're present**. You're at a dinner table to engage in a meal and conversation, not to text message or watch television. The saddest people I know of are those who are on vacation, take their kids to breakfast, and bury their heads in the morning newspaper while their kids play electronic games or listen to music on ear phones. The second saddest people are the couples without kids who do the same thing. The say that when the singing ends, the revolution is over. When the meal talk ends, the relationship is over.

- **Leave the beaten track**. I scuba dive, but not in groups. I pay extra, hire a private dive instructor, and we take our time at interesting sites, not worried about the group tagging along. I mentioned that we received a private tour of the kitchen at Per Se in New York, perhaps the finest restaurant in the country. I've piloted the only B-24 in existence, a World War II aircraft carrier trainer, a Cessna, and the Goodyear Blimp. No, I do not have a pilot's license.

- **Stop "doing" and trust your senses**. We are overwhelmed with potential stimuli today. Watch the scenery. Smell the flowers. Run after the dog. Look at the stars. In all of my life and of all the things I've done, one of the most striking was being lost at night in the Norwegian forests with zero ambient light staring up at a panoply of millions of stars.

- **Use a combination of rigid and loose time frames**. Rigid time frames mean that you should be on time for a performance, finish the meeting you're running at the promised time, give people the amount of time you've promised for an interview or evaluation. Loose time frames mean that you really don't have to go to bed or get up at rigid times, you can stay longer at the park with the kids, and you shouldn't feel guilty about extending a great vacation (never schedule vacations that demand you be somewhere immediately thereafter). In other words, you need to be on time for the plane, but not to leave the pool.

- **"Replay the tapes."** Baseball umpires are taught to do this on close pitches and confusing plays. Ask yourself to re-visualize what you've just seen. It will enable you to enjoy it again, to clarify what it was that caused interest, and to retain it better. Whether you're watching a great performance, seeing your kid play hockey, or watching a daring surfboarder from the beach, try "replaying" what you've just seen. (Many people are so busy trying to find their camera and get it oriented that they lose the entire experience. Some people have seen entire trips only through their camera lenses. Seeing photos is never as good as being there, especially if you were there.)

In grammar school, they teach reading comprehension, and those nasty, politically incorrect generalized tests often measure not just reading speed, but comprehension. ("Speed reading" has never made sense to me at all. "Speed comprehension," however, holds some promise.) Similarly, you have to comprehend what is going on around you, not merely "experience" it.

People whip through museums as if the point were to see as much as possible, irrespective of understanding what it means or implies. The New York Museum of Natural History, The British Museum, The Smithsonian, and The Louvre, would take months to fully appreciate even if one were capable of understanding all of the vast displays and exhibits. Speed reading doesn't help you understand the material better, only to arrive at the end faster. Running through an art gallery, or a state park, or the Appalachian Trail, or an amusement park is no different.

If life is short it's only because we're not paying close attention, we've failed to subjugate and subordinate the alternative demands on our attention, and we've allowed ourselves to become far too easily distracted. We're consumed about "the good old days" or the breakthroughs of the future, rather than the wonder around us. I'm not terribly sympathetic to those who want to preserve green space and wetlands at any cost who do not also bother to enjoy green space and wetlands.

Thriving is about relishing and rejoicing in the present. We are all capable of this singularly existential pursuit.

But attention must be paid.

CHAPTER 6

Mastering your life

Only captains are allowed to walk the quarterdeck

n the British Navy of the 18th and 19th Centuries, only the captain was permitted to walk certain areas on the quarterdeck. Aside from a few others stationed in the general vicinity, such as the helmsman, everyone else needed permission. Even the executive officer, the second in command, ceded the captain his space without trespass.

The captain had earned the right, whether on a brig or ship-of-the line. He had no coaches with him, never delegated the privilege, and was determined to look utterly comfortable there.[39]

Dogs give unconditional love because they seek unlimited treats

We're fond of saying (or at least, I am) that if you want love, get a dog. They are our avatar of unconditional love, despite their owner's age, ethnicity, income, mood, or inclination to watch *Dr. Phil* or *The View*.

At this writing, I've lived with five dogs at close range and it has occurred to me that "unconditional" has some, well, *conditions*. Dogs expect to sleep in the bed, have access to unlimited treats, ride regularly in the car with the windows open, bark at people wearing uniforms, and steal food whenever possible.

---

[39] A surprisingly large number of even senior officers became seasick at sea, given the horrific rolling and pitching of these vessels which had no motive power of their own to maintain headway.

Why wouldn't they give unlimited love? They're living with amusement park owners.

Dogs are more masters of their own life than we are, particularly if you are of the belief that they are non-sentient (I am not of that belief). They readily provide affection and companionship, but clearly seek favors in return, from food to rides, from scratching to toys. They become upset without companionship (which is why you should always have two dogs) and are famous for exhibiting stress due to separation anxiety.

This is not as one-sided as the anthropomorphists would have us believe.

Life is about *quid pro quo*. It is a competitive sport, make no mistakes about that, because if we're good at anything, *it's keeping score*. People change according to what's in their best self-interest—*if they are mentally and emotionally healthy*. If they're not healthy, they'll bend and twist and contort to others' self-interest, and that's not a dance you should be willing to engage in.

How willing and able are you to influence others? If you want to get scratched behind your ear, what are you prepared to offer in return? *Ironically, mastering your life entails helping others to master theirs.* Here are some parameters for creating your own quarterdeck, appreciating the place of others and enabling them to appreciate yours.

Alan's Quarterdeck Perimeter Parameters

- Establish boundaries: What is public and what is personal? What times are you available and what times are for you, alone?

- What decisions do you make, and which are consensual or ceded?

- What are your priorities, which may or may not be shared by others?

- What are your privacy needs? When can you be interrupted? What constitutes a real "emergency"? (I love people who send me email which is marked "highest priority" every time, even if it's forwarding someone else's lame joke. Well, I don't *really* love them.)

- What is the extent of your competence and expertise? The captain knows not only how to fight the ship but also how to provision it. What are you personally accountable for?

- What are you delegating and under what conditions? Can a friend, subordinate, or significant other make certain decisions under certain circumstances?

In other words, specify for those around you what your expectations and preferred operating realities are. I won't argue that you have to compromise at times—after all, you're never a captain on someone else's ship—but we tend to compromise too much and surrender too much without request or provocation.

I'm simply talking, metaphorically, about being captain of your own ship, master of our own fate. We should be prepared to offer a *quid pro quo* in life to further the other person's agenda as well as our own, but we should never put ourselves in a position of sacrificing our own needs to satisfy another's. Even in a marriage or loving relationship, one person constantly surrendering ground to the other doesn't provide for long-term happiness, but rather eventual resentment.

Your quarterdeck is your space in life, where you command and other people respect your space. In fact, they wouldn't dream of encroaching upon it. You neither demand nor provide unconditional love to your human brethren because that is the definition of a skewed relationship. We spend too much time enabling dysfunctional behavior rather than trying to honestly confront and correct it.

Tough love is never easy.

Children can become energy depleters, if you let them. Friends can become overbearing burdens, if you allow it. The best of causes can become time drains, if you don't control your involvement. Aged parents can become chronic, irrational complainers and demanders, if you so enable them.

We must reach an equilibrium in our lives which allows us to deal effectively with our varied relationships on a mutually-healthy basis, though this can often involve some unpleasant confrontation and refusal to bend. When someone is on your ship, they shouldn't intrude on the quarterdeck. And when they are providing what seems like unconditional love, it doesn't require you to respond with unending, infinite support and sustenance.

Dogs are cute and clever, and can eat you out of house and home, chew up what's left, and pretty much mess up the place. We can't allow them to do that, seemingly unconditional love notwithstanding. We have to draw lines and create boundaries.

We have to keep them off our quarterdeck.

You can't be arrested for shooting a passive/aggressive (and if you were, you'd never be convicted)

When my kids were graduating from high school, some of the parents were together at an informal social event. A woman named Molly enquired where my daughter had been admitted to college.

"Syracuse," said my wife, since Danielle was successful in gaining entry into The Newhouse School (with a merit scholarship, no less), arguably the finest school of undergraduate journalism in the land.

"Oh," said Molly, "I assume that was her backup choice?"

On another occasion, when my wife mentioned that I had been acknowledged for something by my alma mater, Rutgers, Molly said amidst the crowd, "Alan went to college?" (I've written more books than Molly has read, and love me or hate me, no one who knows me at all can doubt that I have a formidable education.)

Molly is the stereotypical passive/aggressive. This is a behavior which is rooted in defensiveness and feelings of insecurity. When it is habitual and omnipresent, it becomes pathological.

I've included it here because you cannot master your life if you're unduly phased by passive/aggressives, who constitute one of the most potentially negative behaviors—and blood-suckingly frustrating undermining—that we all encounter. A great deal of the literature points out that these behaviors are often not consciously perpetuated, and that the performers are honestly shocked when confronted.

That has not been my experience. When you confront passive/aggressives with the precise behavior and evidence, they tend to either own up to it or avoid the conversation, realizing that they've been snagged. My experience is that most truly passive/aggressive behavior requires a therapeutic remedy, and no amount of coaching will eliminate the cause, though good, honest, fearless confrontation can adequately mitigate and vitiate the effects.

Here are other manifestations of this behavior. Give some thought to not "if" but "how often" you encounter it:

- Despite promises, deadlines aren't kept and promises are not fulfilled, for no valid reason.

- When a task isn't performed, the individuals state, much too late, that they didn't really agree with the concept, objective, or intent.

- Damning by faint praise: "What a nice speech. You didn't trip walking up there or foul up your opening like you did those first two times."

- Subversive gifts. Example: Giving someone a "Thighmaster" or a gift certificate for a "complete image change" without any comment or context.

- Seemingly innocent undercuts: "That outfit would have looked even better on you two years ago."

- Worrisome observations: "Your baby's crying seems manic. You know, they have identified bipolarism even in infants."

You get the idea. Just as energy suckers can steal the very breath out of you, passive/aggressives can suck the very lifeblood out of you. You cannot allow these people to influence your actions in any way, and you can't surrender more than 30 seconds to dealing with them.

The most efficacious counterattack should blunt them forever onward. Since they cannot tolerate confrontation on their actual (as opposed to pseudo-) intent, and you don't want to engage in their games, here is what you say:

- "Why would you say something so personally hurtful? Surely you realize how inappropriate that comment is?"

- "You're giving me advice that assumes I'm damaged in some way. Is that what you believe? Why would you think that?"

- "I've always treated you with respect and the assumption that you are healthy and supportive of others. Why are you acting so unhealthy and unsupportive in these comments?"

- "Have I done something to you inadvertently that causes you to say such disrespectful things? I thought we had a good and honest relationship."

- "Whether or not you now disagree with the intent—which you never bothered to mention in the prior month while I was relying on you—you've now undermined me and this endeavor by not meeting your personal accountabilities, and that means I can't ever trust you again."

- "I've been acting on the basis of mutual trust and respect, but now I find that your comments and behavior will not allow that to continue. Why have you chosen to violate our trust?"

If these are accusatory, so be it. All passive/aggressives' behaviors are about them, not you. They are about degrading others since they feel incapable of elevating themselves. But it's not an irresistible force and you can be an immovable object.

The major problem is that so many people can't recognize the passive/aggressive pathology confronting them, so they extend courtesies, act forgiving, provide latitude, and worst of all, think that they are the ones who must change.

You won't get arrested for "shooting down" a passive/aggressive with the honest, confronting techniques suggested here, and no jury of your peers would ever convict you, anyway. But I guarantee that if you're moved to attempt rehabilitation, or forgiveness, or tolerance, you will have surrendered a mile for the inch they are seeking. You cannot master your life when you allow others to undermine it.

And the last person you want on the quarterdeck is someone who promised to turn the wheel when you asked, but has decided that perhaps they won't follow orders after all if they can make you look bad.

**There is nothing as stupid as emailing with your thumbs
(unless it's walking around with a pulsing, blue light in your ear)**

Two stories:

Story #1

I was asked to meet an attorney in an upscale bar in Atlanta to discuss the possibility of doing work with his firm. I was told that he was the progressive partner, and that his partners wouldn't want him to even discuss improvements to the structure and billing practices; hence, the bar.

He told me by phone he'd be five minutes late and to have a drink, and to order him a martini. I don't have to be given such instructions twice from a cicerone, and I was duly sipping my 42 Below vodka, which had only glanced at a vermouth label.

Two minutes or so late, in strides the attorney with a blinking, blue light in his ear. He walked over (recognized my table by the two-martini, one-person anomaly) shook my hand, sat down, and took a sip, muttering "cheers." I waited for the blue thing to be removed or disgorged. It remained.

He began speaking about the firm and his stubborn partners, and that he was told I was bold enough to wade in if he could wangle it. I stepped in after the fifth sentence.

"You have to remove the blue thing," I said, "because you're not going to be taking calls while we're meeting, I hope, and frankly it's so disconcerting that I can't focus on what you're saying."

He removed it with something between a smirk and a grimace.

We never did work together.

Story #2

I was attending a speakers' convention and playing hooky, strolling through the hotel lobby, when I happened across a long-time acquaintance. I had helped this person through several tough aspects of his career, our wives had met, and we had shared dinner on a couple of occasions.

"Alan," he said, "I need to get your reaction to something that happened to me yesterday."

"Sure," I said.

"A client called, and made an unusual request. He...."

At that point, he was interrupted by his cell phone ringing.

"Excuse me," he said without waiting, and turned slightly to his right.

"Oh, Richie," he exclaimed, "I've been waiting to talk to you. Can you give me a quick summary of the meeting you had last week with the contractor?"

As he continued listening, I continued walking.

My moral here is that you use technology to master your fate, not run it, let alone ruin it.[40]

I ran a series of strategy sessions for a $1.5 billion firm, which included the CEO and top five officers. They were all officially armed with BlackBerrys, and we had an agreement that they couldn't text or check email during the sessions. But every break, lunch, and other excuse was utilized for the crazy, spasmodic thumb scrolling and clicking that marks the addict these days.

---

[40] I could get cute here and say when you insert "I" into technology you go from running it to ruining it, but I won't. There may be no "I" in "team," but there is one in "win."

How did people run companies prior to constant technological inter-ruption? Pretty well, as far as I can see, certainly no worse than today. One of the seminal books describing how it was done was *In Search of Excellence*, not *In Search of a Connection*.

There is a fallacy that constantly being in touch somehow demonstrates control, or quality, or leadership. All it really demonstrates is zealotry and an inability to understand how to maximize the true advantages of technology. And the downside, of course, is missing something in the present or alienating someone in front of you. (Once you take a phone call while you're with someone, assuming that your wife isn't going into labor and you're not a brain surgeon on call, you're telling the people in proximity that they are a lower priority than an unknown phone call. You'll see equal rudeness when a salesperson or cashier or ticket agent makes you wait to pick up a ringing phone. If a concierge ever does that to you, it's time to find a better hotel.)

If you want to master your life:

- Deal with the people with you and near you as if they are valued or don't deal with them at all.

- Never allow mobile devices to interrupt your day or your travels unless you're expecting a truly important call.

- Don't deal with business and personal concerns in public. You'll lose respect and effectiveness.

- Stop appearing as a pack horse or the equivalent of a low level minion with a pocket protector: Ditch the phone holster, the ear piece, the pocketed phone with ear buds, the PDA while you're walking. Get a grip, and I don't mean on a PDA.

- Understand that constant connection and frequent updates are not necessarily better ways to manage or lead, but can manage to lead you astray.

I'm not impressed by an attorney who feels constrained to leave metal in his ear, nor a "friend" who turns a deaf ear.

Dumping the primary baggage
and getting even with your parents

Our parents raise us, and eventually become our children, if we all live long enough. We need to recognize that the same thing will happen to us, so it may be best right now to cut your kid some slack about the text messaging or curfew hour, or you may find yourself without your favorite "Billy Joel in Concert" tapes or poached pears when you're in the home.

Our parents don't merely raise us, they inculcate us, advertently and inadvertently. Their shrugs and moans represent some kind of Gnostic wisdom which accretes in our cerebral cortex like stalactites and stalagmites, until it's tough wending our way through the passages without bumping our heads or stubbing out toes. When the inevitable shrink asks us, "How do you feel about that?" we're more than likely to reply with what our parents told us to think about that.

How do you feel about that?

Our primary baggage, lying around the hallways so that we trip over it whenever we think we're on our way to Thriving, comprises our upbringing and nurturing. If you're told you're clumsy and tend to trip over chalk lines, you probably are not going to gravitate toward stardom in dance or athletics. However, if you're told you have a great musical sense and pleasing voice, you may well overcome the slings and arrows of the "in crowd" and develop your abilities in the school band.

For something like 20 years—and for many people, a great deal longer—parents and influential relatives and siblings paint our pictures for us. More often that not, as adults, we need to dispose of a great deal of the art work.

But you can't merely drop baggage. If you simply drop it next to you on the train of life, due to the 15th Law of Thermodynamics or Schroedinger's Cat or something, it continues, there at your side, to move at the same speed you do. *You must throw the luggage off the train, into the countryside.*

Don't be afraid to bean a passing cow.

I've seen parents who should have their licenses revoked create these types of scenarios:

- You can't be successful enough: "That a fine grade, but not as good as Dorothy's, or even last year's, is it?"

- My gift is for your weakness: "I thought this gift certificate would help buy some more stylish clothing."

- The sacrifice sacrifice: "If you want to throw away all of my work and investment in trying to help you...."

- We're all in this together: "We need to show the Smiths that they're not the only ones who can have a starting player on the varsity team."

- The "So what?" rhetorical: "You mean that you're actually paid to write for a publication like that?"

- Those were the days: "Very nice—of course they've weakened the standards so much in the last few years."

You get the idea. But what you may not get is that there is a time in your life when it becomes *your responsibility* to jettison the old art work. It's not unusual to see an otherwise successful adult continue to be cowed, controlled, and cajoled by an overbearing parent. This stuff can last forever. (And if your parents are well off and planned well, it's not even up to you to decide if they get the poached pears in the home.)

If you want to Thrive, you must get rid of ancient, inaccurate, and often malicious stereotypes and mores which subliminally are guiding your growth (or lack thereof). Your parents (and their memory) are to be revered and maintained as appropriate, but not their commandments nor constraints. Even the best-intentioned parents can implant time-delay fuses which burst a bubble on a special occasion, an achievement, or a life change. Those screaming soccer moms and Little League dads, though ostensibly cheering their kid on, are more likely cheering for themselves and creating destructive role models. (A few too many people have been killed, hurt, and jailed at kids' athletic competitions. I'm just waiting for the dance recital brawls.)

The mother who insisted that a less (or more) sexy prom dress be worn; the father who said that mechanical ability was just not a possibility in you; the older brother who maintained that his shoes would always be too big for you; the over-achieving sister who never said a word but just outperformed everything you tried; the cousin in Long Island who always had it better and knew how to act better than you: All of these familial denizens have left their spore in the cave of your life.

Leave the cave and buy a nice condo on the water.

Here are questions to ask yourself, to help you Thrive. If you can't honestly grapple with them, find therapeutic help. ("Life coaches" are generally worthless at this stuff. Who certifies the certifiers? Find someone who is really skilled in the area.)[41]

1. List your beliefs about yourself, pro and con. Then ask, "What is my evidence to support this belief?" For example, if you feel you have no musical ability, ask if you've ever even tried taking voice

---

[41] A well-known "life coach" made famous by appearances on syndicated TV shows, founded her own coaching magazine which promptly named her "coach of the year." When she wanted to thank me for helping teach her aspects of the coaching business, she sent me a card telling me: "State your desire three times a day and it will come true." (It must work, since my desire was that she would get away from me.) You can't make this stuff up. That was her methodology!

or instrument lessons in the recent past. If you believe you're a great writer, ask if you've had anything commercially published.[42]

2. What is the current feedback you receive from contemporaries, especially people who *do not* know you well? Is it consistent with your self-beliefs, or different? If the latter, why?

3. Ask yourself what your most delimiting, undermining, constricting beliefs about yourself are, and determine what you can do to change or overcome them. For example, if you feel you can't speak well in public, join Toastmasters, a very low-threat, comfortable remedy.

4. Choose some important beliefs you'd like to have about yourself, e.g., you're a great listener. Then make that happen through application. For example, attend a meeting where you deliberately do not ask questions or provide your viewpoint, but merely listen and respond non-verbally.

Dump the baggage, before it dumps you and the train races away into the night, leaving you and the cow.

Creating baggage and getting even with your kids

You can look at kids as simply immature parents. On their way to giving baggage to their progeny, they'll practice by giving baggage to you.

I've always felt that parents who don't intervene when their baby is crying, or don't stop their child from running around the store bothering other people, or don't discourage their teen from trying drugs and alcohol so as not to "confine them," are simply too lazy or scared to make the hard choices required of mature adults.

Sometimes, your kids are wrong and need correction. Sometimes they are very wrong and need a lesson.

---

[42] You challenge positive beliefs to ensure they are true so that they can be exploited.

No captain walked the quarterdeck with his kids at his feet. Sometimes you need a strong dose of "healthy selfishness." Sacrificing for your kids is shortchanging them, because you will either grow to resent them, or become the parent cited above ("If you want to throw away all I've done for you...."), or both. You put your own oxygen mask on first. (More about that in the next chapter.) You make sure you're healthy. You establish comfort for yourself.

All that will help your kids.

We all take baggage on our trips, and the journey through life should be no different. I'm simply espousing getting rid of the stuff you can't—or, more importantly, shouldn't—be wearing any more. The stuff you retain should be age-appropriate, comfortable, practical, long-lived, and attractive.

We all grow by exploiting strengths, not by correcting weakness (which is why so many "self-help" books are useless). But the strengths need to be identified, codified, and replicated. Unless we know *why* we're good, it's very hard to replicate the behavior. ("That was a great meeting, thank you!" "You're welcome!" But what was so great about it? What do you make sure to do again next time?)

Here's how you create "positive baggage," which no one much talks about:

- **Find out what's comfortable and works**. If you are best running a meeting by interaction, then use a minimalist agenda. If you prefer a strict order, than use a detailed agenda.

- **Give yourself options, based on the climate**. Try to never leave yourself with "take it or leave it" alternatives. If you're not sure about the desirability of a social function, then go, but have an excuse ready if you have to leave or ask someone to call you at a certain time in case you need the excuse to leave.

- **Travel light**. Positive baggage should weigh a lot less than negative baggage, with all its insinuation, history, and obligation. Just as you build on strength, you also build best on your best strengths. Always be clear as to what the "point on your arrow" is, so that you have aerodynamics and not a flying barn. Change the event to your house, or talk to your kid's teacher with some prepared questions, or practice saying, "I don't know yet, but answer a few questions and I'll be able to find out" when you feel cornered.

- **Have your tools of choice available**. Don't use the other person's field, equipment, rules, and officials, or you're going to lose the game. Meet on at least common or neutral ground. If you're asked for something, it's perfectly healthy and acceptable to ask for something in return. *Remember, the people who are challenged to a duel have their choice of weapons.*

- **Don't accept others' baggage**. I referred to time management expert Bill Oncken and his monkeys earlier. The only thing worse than your own negative baggage is other people's negative baggage. You can only carry so much, and if you're overloaded you might just drop your best outfits.

We all carry baggage through life. The idea is to make sure it's positive, supportive, and attractive for our intent and journey. We can't allow parents or kids to give us theirs or even to influence our own. That may sound selfish, but you can't fit into others' outfits and, even if you could, you'd probably look foolish.

The opposite of those parents who allow their kids to run wild are those who embrace their kids in a democratic relationship of mutual learning and somewhat unequal feedback. You know more than your kids and you have to enforce certain rules, for their own protection, for the public's well being, and for your own sanity. But you can learn from them, deciding what baggage to take on for yourself.

If you haven't caught on by now, the objective is to weed through and greatly reduce your parents' contribution to your baggage, and to create your own with the appropriate influence of child rearing (and friends, intimate relationships, social activities, civic responsibilities, professional obligations, and so on). "Old" baggage is almost always moldy and forlorn, unusable except as a nag, weight, and guilt mechanism. The baggage you create is always fresh, renewable, and relevant. It's built on what you want to be, not what you used to be, or worse, what someone else wanted you to be.

If you seek to Thrive, the one thing you can least afford is *victimhood* and its attendant *poverty mentality*. We'll turn to that next, and throw it the hell off the train.

Let the cows beware!

CHAPTER 7

If the alternative is victimhood, then choose to be the oppressor

Slaying the poverty mentality

ncreasingly, I meet people who are convinced that the world has transpired against them. Their parents left them a poor legacy; their bosses were unappreciative of their talents[43]; they metabolically can't master a skill (or have ADD, or longitudinal daydream syndrome—LDS—so something); or the fates have cast them a cruel blow. It's a conspiracy right up there with the grassy knoll, Hangar 52, and the UN is taking over. (I'm waiting for the secretary general of the UN to welcome a UFO on the grassy knoll and knock a few of these off at one time.)

I was talking to a woman interested in being coached, who insisted that I understand that she was let go from three consecutive positions because of politics, or downsizing, or the economy, or whatever.

In turning her down, I mentioned that if she were *really* valuable to her firms, she wouldn't be allowed to leave, and I wasn't going to help her avoid reality by blaming "them."

---

[43] By far, the most egregious case of this can be seen in Mensa, which I joined just to see how hard it is to become part of the "top two percent" of the brainy. (It isn't.) Nowhere else have I encountered so many smug people who claim their "gifts" weren't appreciated by dumber superiors, educators, and colleagues, and so they are not more successful than they are. If you're so "gifted," shouldn't you be able to overcome the slings and arrows of outraged inferiors? Not if you're simply a professional victim, and belong to an association that encourages it.

Put your own oxygen mask on first

This is one of those clichés that I've truly come to like and respect: You can't help others until you help yourself. Recovering alcoholics can help those still wrestling with the bottle only if they, themselves, have been helped. It's tough to do *pro bono* work or charity work if you need every minute of time to generate cash to keep your family from starving.

I want the airplane's cockpit crew to get the oxygen first, so that they can ensure my safety. I can then reach for mine and thereafter try to help someone else.

There are all kinds of very effective and accurate apothegms which guide us to charitable works, helping our neighbors, and sacrifice. Fair enough, but you still have to have something left over.

Would you rather have a highly successful surgeon, with many patients and experience, working on you, or someone who is brand new to the procedure? Would you choose an attorney who was cheaper but never handled a similar case to yours, or a more expensive one with a track record of 93 percent success with cases such as yours? If you choose your food and dining merely by low cost, you're going to have poor nourishment and profound indigestion.

There are people with a professional poverty mentality, a perpetual victimhood. The "man" or the "bureaucracy," or "the company," or the "inner circle" won't allow them to enter or succeed. Here are a few ironies:

- When country clubs routinely denied entry to Jews purely on the basis of religion, the Jews went out and built their own (often more lavish) country clubs. They turned those who make them outcasts into outcasts themselves.

- In many African-American communities, where it is claimed that work and individual initiative are hard to come by given the circumstances of ghettos, local stores have opened and Thrived run by Koreans, who have a cultural belief system of hard work and family discipline. (In fact, studies report that black immigrants from Africa and the Caribbean see America as a land of opportunity and tend to succeed more than native-born blacks who receive an indoctrination of victimhood.)

- Many inner city schools are turning around kids' lives and turning out great students who are college bound, because insightful and dedicated educators have formed new learning experiences and created different governance for the schools. There is nary a cry against City Hall, the unions, or the school board to be heard, because they are irrelevant, and such cries don't work in any case.

- Forget the people who were born on third base and think they've hit a triple. We all meet or see people daily who started with nothing or less (they were in debt) and rose to become successful. *That's because they didn't allow their circumstances to become their excuse.*

I was parking my car in Providence one afternoon when I noticed a man standing with a used soda cup outside of a McDonald's soliciting passersby for change. As I watched, another man walked up, they chatted, looked at their watches, and the beggar emptied his cup and then handed it to the second man, who proceeded to beseech people entering and leaving the store.

I had happened along amidst a shift change!

You can bemoan the past and the mistakes lodged and collected on its shelves until the end of time, but it's not going to help you tomorrow. In free societies, all that's needed to Thrive are a belief that you can succeed; the discipline and work ethic required to succeed; and the resilience to keep trying in all kinds of weather. Please don't tell me you need an outfielder to drop the ball, or a walk to first base, or for the pitcher to hit you. As my frustrated Little League coaches used to bellow at us: "Swing the bat! You're not going to get on base unless you swing the bat!"

I guarantee that if you refuse to get in the game because of real or (more often) perceived injustices, you'll never get to first base. You'll just be an observer, drinking beer in the stands and cheering for guys making millions more than you are.

So take care of yourself, put on the awaiting oxygen mask first:

- **Provide yourself with "space" and time, to think, meditate, enjoy, ponder**. Don't sacrifice all of your personal time to the family or outside obligations.

- **Spend money on yourself.** You need to dress well if you're to be taken seriously. You need decent accessories. You ought to be well groomed: Hair, makeup, skin care, and so on.

- **Find things to enjoy and time to enjoy them**. Go to a show. Watch your favorite TV programs. Develop and pursue hobbies. Get instruction in sailing or golf or handicrafts so that you improve and can enjoy them even more.

- **Keep personally fit**. Get an annual physical. Join a gym and consider a personal trainer. Purchase a bike or exercise equipment. Take care of yourself.

- **Manage your relationships well**. Either "fix" or abandon those that chronically do not work. Don't allow yourself to be someone else's punching bag or emotional bombing target.

- **Gain clarity.** Convince yourself that you can't help your kids, your siblings, or your parents unless you are operating from a position of relative strength, financially, psychologically, and emotionally. Don't let others lay "guilt trips" on you, and don't create them for yourself. (More on this later.)

- **Treat yourself**. Buy something on impulse. Get something that prompts others to notice and remark. It isn't illegal, immoral, or inappropriate. It's simply making a difference for yourself.

If you put on your own oxygen mask first, you can start helping others and you'll feel far less like a victim. Victims aren't able to help others very well. But people who are breathing easily on their own can start doing anything they please.

Ultimately, *being willing to take the actions to treat yourself with respect and dignity is the first step in being a true philanthropist.*

Eschew others' guilt

There are people who make a living by lading guilt onto others' ships. Some do it deliberately, some inadvertently, but the effect is devastating no matter the motive.

The voyage becomes a guilt trip.

Parents and children, as noted above, are prime sources, but so are other family members, colleagues, friends and business associates. Why does this happen with such regularity?

Let's define "guilt": It is the belief that one is culpable, responsible for some wrongdoing. It is cognitive ("I recognize and believe it") as well as emotional ("I feel it") and it involves both moral and legal infraction. There are degrees of response to guilt, from regret over being late, to devastation over a failed relationship. To assuage guilt, people often ask if one has "remorse," which is a sort of secular penance for the guilt. (Does football player Michael Vick, who served prison time for cruelty to dogs, have remorse, or did he simply serve his time? Who's to know?)

We create our own guilt often enough, from violating overarching standards others set for us to considering ourselves sinners who need constant forgiveness. I'm not talking here about self-created guilt. I'm talking about what we accept too readily from others (that often re-sults in self-perpetuated guilt).

Guilt can have a positive aspect. It serves as both personal and social control, in that it can discourage personal and socially adverse behav-iors. It may stop people from stealing that which is readily stolen or prompt them to contribute to a cause.

But, in my view, the negative aspect of guilt is not terribly different from the effects of depression, in that it dampens and masks talent. Guilty people are constantly trying to atone, or to beat themselves up, or deny themselves, or sacrifice in the name of others. I spoke to a very successful, talented woman who was pursuing an unwise and unprofit-able business venture. After quite a bit of coaching I found out that the business was based on intellectual property she had purchased. At the time of purchase, she promised the seller she would "take care of"—in perpetuity—the people who were dependent on his prior venture.

Thus, she produced materials and provided support to adults who should have been able to help themselves, who were a drain on her energy and resources, but for whom she felt responsible. She felt guilty even thinking about abandoning these people.

This operates on all levels. I was asked to coach an executive vice presi-dent who was profane, a bully, and belligerent in public. I determined he was not salvageable and needed to be removed. The president told me that he couldn't let the guy go or even require counseling because he had promised the prior owner of the company—this guy's father—that he would "always take care of him." The guilt of not doing so nearly ruined the entire operation.[44]

---

[44] I managed to get rid of him by convincing the president that the employees interpreted the aberrant behavior as endorsed by the president, since he did nothing to stop it. That was intolerable, so the subordinate had to go.

Why do people allow guilt to be thrust upon them by others? I think for these reasons:

- We evaluate ourselves in terms of how well others accept us and we fear not being accepted, so we contort ourselves into strange positions to avoid being rejected.

- Our self-esteem is low or fragile. We feel that others' requests are reasonable and that our sacrifice is minor—in fact, selfish, if we refuse.

- We fail to engage in healthy selfishness—the personal oxygen mask—because we have been inculcated with the mysticism that we should go last, let others indulge before us, and that we should never take the first or largest piece.

- We mistake capitulation for empathy. It's fine to understand how someone else feels, but their problem or misfortune or need shouldn't require us to surrender to it.

If you want to eschew others' guilt catapults, consider the following in order to Thrive:

1. **Question all requests for obligation**. "Will you take care of my colleagues?" should generate this response: "What does that have to do with a good deal for the both of us? If that's a deal breaker, then we may not have a deal." Don't blindly accept these requests as though they are minor issues.

2. **Evaluate obligations in terms of scope and duration**. Taking care of your brother for life (he becomes an adult at some point), helping coach the soccer team (a season is three months long), and helping with a committee report (which should take an hour) are three different things, with varying degree of obligation.

3. **Lance the issue**. If your guilt is about neglecting someone, schedule a lunch once a month so there is regular contact. If your guilt is about not giving enough to charitable causes, create a monthly deduction from your check. If your guilt is about something you did years ago which can never be undone, then compensate for it in another way (and consider therapeutic help).[45]

4. **Confront the launcher**. Ask why they insist on trying to make you feel guilty. "Oh, I assure you I would never do that," should be rebutted with, "Then why do you choose to tell me that if I don't agree to do this no one else will and I'll be to blame?" You enable guilt-invokers by accepting their flawed reasoning, no less than buying an alcoholic a flask of whiskey.

5. **Remove yourself or ignore the launcher**. Everyone has to deal with their mother, but you neither have to accept the guilt nor argue about it. You can either refuse the conversation or ignore the requests and innuendo. I remember sitting in first class on the Acela high speed train one summer, when a scantily-clad woman in short-shorts, low-cut blouse, strappy sandals, and nothing else complained that she was "cold," and the steward went to the control panel, but didn't seem to touch anything. When he returned I pointed out that no one reasonably attired in the car was cold. "Oh, I didn't actually change the setting," he confided, "I just pretended to." Later she thanked him and told him she was much more comfortable.[46]

---

[45] Note that the "guilt of not having enough" is not mentioned here! "Guilt" that your companions are doing better than you are is self-imposed and just a variety of "there is always a bigger boat." See Chapter 10.

[46] I've seen bartenders make "very dry" martinis by ignoring the vermouth altogether and still have people complain it was not dry enough. They'd simply return the same drink and the patron would express gratitude that "this is much better."

6. **Get some help**. I'm a big believer in therapy, particularly when it is undertaken from a position of confidence and strength. Some guilt isn't easily surfaced, because someone else buried it in you years ago. Some guilt that is surfaced is tough to deal with unless we can understand the cause and our own role in perpetuating it. In these cases, a learned third-party is a great investment. (Just don't feel guilty about seeing a therapist! Some of the healthiest people visit therapists regularly during various periods of their lives.)

Only a psychopath has a complete absence of guilt. I'm not suggesting any such pristine (or disassociative) state. I am suggesting that we are often surrounded by people who are trying to load guilt on us, and that such guilt is paralyzing and dysfunctional.

Why wouldn't you want to combat that? No one Thrives when they go through life feeling guilty and having that guilt stoked every day so that we're always feeling the heat.

"Attention must be paid" and the tragedy of Willy Loman

When Arthur Miller's iconic salesman, Willy Loman, dies, having worked himself to death with techniques made obsolescent by time and youth, his colleagues largely ignore his passing. His distraught wife, failing to gain their sympathies, shouts: "Attention must be paid!" It's not an elegant or even very grammatical phrase. But it's extraordinarily powerful and poignant.

Our victimhood is often the result of our failure to break out of our own self-imposed prisons or to venture from our carefully cushioned nests. "I have often reflected," said Niccolo Machiavelli, "that the causes of the successes or failures of men depend upon their manner of suiting their conduct to the times."

There is very little new under the sun, insofar as our interactions, behaviors, and reactions are concerned. But technology, the economy, and society do constantly shift and alter, and our manner of suiting our conduct to those three moving targets makes a huge difference in our ability to Thrive. Willy Loman continued to try a "shoeshine and a smile" long after his old friends and buddies had disappeared, and the competition became tougher, price became king, and business began to trump relationships.

The attention that must be paid to Willy Loman's death isn't merely for a hard working man who couldn't adjust to the times and for whom loyalty could not overcome business results. The attention is for all of us to examine our behaviors and avoid Willy's mistakes, avoid his insularity, avoid his obsession with routine.

A recent news column addressed a *New York Times* reporter's story of overspending and coming close to losing his home in the economic turbulence of early 2009. He admitted he should have known better, was distraught that he and his wife (who also worked) might lose their home because of being over-leveraged and over-spending.

So, of course, he wrote a book about it, which the columnist was plugging for a colleague in the ink trade, and if it sells well enough, he'll have his money and then some. The problems, however, are these:

- He *did not* include in the book the fact that his wife had declared bankruptcy *on two previous occasions*. In both cases she spent more than she earned and had no other recourse. He commented to the columnist that, "If I had to do it over again, I would have included this history, but at the time I didn't want to put my wife through more hurt." Oh.

- He is accountable. The columnist tried to make the point that the rapacious lenders and credit card companies caused the writer's sad state of affairs, but no one forced the credit on him and no one put a gun to his head and insisted he spend it.

- The columnist's ultimate point was what we hear all too often today: It's "them." Don't worry, don't be too hard on yourself, "they" are to blame. That is the ultimate in the crazed early 21st art form known as "victimology."

The media instruct us in how to be victims. It's easy being a victim, after all, since victims have no accountability. The problem is twofold:

1. This demeans true victims, people herded to gas chambers, hanged for their race, deprived of basic health care, murdered by terrorists. They had no recourse, they were not accountable, they didn't deserve their fate.

2. Victimology can be claimed by everyone with surprising results. I found myself one night at the home of a man whose property dated from a charter granted after the war—the Revolutionary War—and the charter was signed by King George III. He could buy and sell me perhaps 100 times over. But he took a shine to me for some reason, and at the end of the evening said, "Alan, if you ever need me, I'm here, because it's us against them." On the way home my wife asked why I looked so puzzled. "If he and I are 'us,' then who are 'them'?" I wondered.

If you're a victim, you're never in control. While you may not be culpable, you're also not responsible. If you had to choose antipodal positions, then be an "oppressor," *if that means taking control of your life and trying to influence those around you to meet your personal objectives.*

You can't Thrive by complaining.

You don't stand out in a crowd by encouraging people to pity you.

You don't gather followers or truly influence others by claiming you're powerless.

"Attention must be paid" to the attempts to foist victimhood upon us, by the media which sees itself as a victim; [47] by the self-help gurus who want to flatten your abs and shrink your brain; by the incessant clamoring of the mediocre who take solace in bringing others down to their level instead of trying to elevate themselves; and by the failing primary and secondary educational systems which are totally focused on the providers (teachers) and not the customers (students).

Willy Loman died fighting for his life in a world that had changed to the extent that his weapons and techniques were no longer valid. He couldn't change. He didn't understand why "they" were doing this to him.

Don't ask for favors, demand your due

It's unusual to get through a week without someone asking me for a favor who doesn't realize that's what the transaction is really about. They don't think they're asking a favor, or they pretend that it's just a normal exchange. Examples just on the business side:

- Go to their website, review their text and appeal, and give them some feedback. (Among other services, I do that for a living.)

- Give them an introduction to some of my clients because they "need" what the purveyor has.

- Meet with them so that they can "pick my brain."

- Allow them to publish extensive works I've created on their website, with all due attribution so that they can increase traffic.

---

[47] Newspapers, in particular, whine about the Internet when the truth is that they've never had the initiative or innovation to handle alternative information sources dating back to the advent of radio. Today, broadcast media are losing viewers and blame everything except the true cause: dull programming and plastic people who can't keep up with the times. Do we really need $500,000 news anchors who say, "Between you and I"?

- Send them a book, CD, or download for free, or give them a scholarship to attend a workshop.[48]

- Allow them to "tag along" so that they can learn my approaches and, of course, appropriate them.

On the personal side:

- Change my schedule to accommodate theirs because they want to improve their condition without regard to the possibility that it deteriorates mine.

- Give them a key contact for a favor which they'll abuse and not repay.

- Request that I pay a higher proportionate share because they are temporarily short of cash, or I had a tad more than they did, or I make more than they do.

- Spend more time and money than would be necessary elsewhere because they are "friends."

Now, before you conclude I'm an insensitive lout and oppressor, let me tell you why I won't feed this poverty mentality. No one should expect favors. No one should be begging for help. They can always offer something *of real value* as at least a passing attempt at a *quid pro quo*, and an admission that they are, indeed, asking for help.

On the business side, value you can offer:

- Introductions to buyers or recommenders.

- Tickets to a sporting or entertainment event.

- Legwork or research from a project you're running.

---

[48] I provide scholarships to almost every single workshop I run, some as high as $15,000, but *never* to anyone who asks for one.

- Proofreading or product fulfillment.

- Technical or financial expertise (if that's their expertise, of course).

- Positive book reviews, testimonials, and so on.

On the personal side, value you can offer:

- Take care of the property—mow the lawn, paint something.

- Give me the better seats or position.[49]

- Provide an unexpected favor or gift at some point.

- Help out with my kids or pets (recommend a school or a vet).

- Merely formally thank me (the "thank you" note has disappeared, despite the catalogs from all those companies selling personalized notes!).

You get the idea. But *they* should have the idea proactively.

Every time someone has requested "collaboration" with me, by the way, what they really want to do is take money out of my pocket and put it into their own, They never come with business on the table, or with value, or with anything but the vague conceptual belief that they will be better off if they can hang around with me. (Only one such offer was ever tendered with a firm piece of business that the other consultant needed me to help with, and we made over $100,000 together delivering the project. That's one time in over 25 years, or let's even say 15 years since my brand has been at this level.)

The moral of the story is that you can't Thrive by being a beggar and you can't Thrive by feeding beggars. Remember the shift change of

---

[49] For years, at a very expensive dinner everyone knew I was paying for, someone would get there early and take the best seats at the table. My wife and I would wind up in spare chairs at the end. Finally, I sent my daughter to stake out the place and take care of the seating.

the begging cup outside of a McDonald's? The beggars are pros. Feed them and they come to work every day and often draw others.

If demanding that people "pay to play" means you're an "oppressor," then get good at it. I can offer people scholarships when I choose and provide *pro bono* work when I choose because I have the means to do so. I have the means because I don't allow others to "take" from me out of some misguided sense of philanthropy.

Conversely, while you shouldn't ask for favors, you should demand your "due." By that I mean:

- Don't provide free help in areas in which you normally are paid if the person asking can clearly afford to pay you.

- Reiterating, the Bible states that, while forgiving is required, putting yourself in a position where the harm or affront will be repeated is not required nor expected (nor rational). Don't allow someone who has burned you to light another match in your presence.

- Demand credit when and where due. If you're overlooked (whether deliberately nor not, the effect is the same despite the cause), make it clear what you provided, supplied, or created. Wall flowers are not chosen as centerpieces. Humility is a wonderful concept, but it shouldn't include martyrdom.[50]

- Don't be overwhelmed by the high and the mighty (or, more commonly, the loud and the haughty). The more you subordinate yourself, the more you enable the true oppressors. You can't cook as well on the back burner and you can't drive at all from the back seat. Grab the controls when you want to steer the conversation or the issue.

---

[50] One of the great quotes on the subject by humorist George Ade: "Don't pity the martyrs, they love the work."

Don't choose to be a victim, either by engaging in the activities or allowing others to engage in them with you, making you a victim. Enabling victims is infectious and you become one of them. For example, psychologically, when you hate someone, when you're extremely angry with them and can't let it go, you've become their slave. Your enslavement is worse, in most cases, than the original transgression's ill effects! The mosquito bite which you keep scratching doesn't go away, as it would if ignored or medicated, but becomes a far worse, festering infection which you continue to pick at.

Okay, not pretty, but pretty accurate, right?

When you are infuriated that someone has taken advantage of you, you begin the "shoulda" nonsense that starts the process of wishing your life away:

- "I should have told her off."

- "I never should have allowed him to shut me down."

- "I wish I would have replied with...."

- "I wish I had a second chance to...."

Fill in the "shoulda" with anything—it doesn't matter. It's too late and you're still beating yourself up worse than the other person had probably originally intended.

Why do about 99 percent of people pass by beggars on the street, even though most of them have the means right in their pocket to help? Is it because they are bad people, or preoccupied, or embarrassed? I don't think so. I think it's because they either don't believe the beggar needs to be there, or they resent the fact that this is what they've chosen for themselves.

Harsh? Perhaps. But what about the figurative beggars in your life? Do you believe that, personally or professionally, they really deserve the free help, the upper hand, the benefit of the doubt, the extra effort?

Do you believe that what they've chosen to do—impinge on your time, finances, energy, and perhaps good name—is the proper choice for them, or could they have chosen something different?

Nothing is stopping any of us from proactively offering aid to any person or cause. I do it all the time, and the surprise on the other end is part of my gratification. (I told a person who gave me an unexpected gift that he really didn't have to do it. "I know," he said, "that's why I did it.") I'm simply suggesting that Thriving is about that initiative, about that choice, about that personal decision.

Such generosity shouldn't be thrust on you or expected by others.

If you want to truly Thrive, don't ask for favors and don't mindlessly grant them. This has nothing to do with being "nice" or "polite" or "appropriate." It has everything to do with living a successful, prosperous, contributing life. You can't do that as a victim or surrounded by victims.

Talent always outs

In the long run, at the end of the day, when you boil it all away, the bottom line, (insert your appropriate bromide here: _____), talent will always "out." That means that talent eventually overcomes conniving, subterfuge, manipulation, machination, and luck.

Or, as the actor with a rather tragic life, Montgomery Clift, observed, "When you're good, they can't get at you."

The reason is that our society and capitalist system prize competence. As I mentioned in an earlier discussion, if you keep getting downsized, removed, or turned down for promotion by "politics," or "bad timing," or lousy luck, you're probably not all that valuable—not all that good. If you were, they couldn't afford to let you go. Sorry, but the Chicago Bulls would not have cut Michael Jordan, and the symphony won't lose Yo-Yo Ma through RIF (reduction in force).

In the words of the world of athletics, you have to become a "franchise player."

Moreover, the road to self-esteem is paved with competence. Even though efficacy (ability to do things well) and self-worth (ability to feel good about yourself no matter how you do) can be independent variables, they can affect each other. The more competent you are and the more talents you can apply, the better your rate of success. The better your rate of success, the better you feel about yourself, and the more likely you are to invest in gaining still more competence and tools. That's the wonderful "Thrive cycle" you can enter if you so choose. [51]

The Thrive cycle

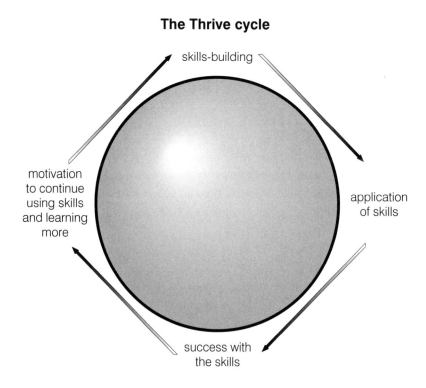

skills-building

motivation to continue using skills and learning more

application of skills

success with the skills

[51] My thanks to Drs. Bob Cohen and Terry Giblin, for their insights into discussions of self-esteem throughout the book.

The figure on the previous page shows very simply how this operates. Skills lead to application, which creates success, which provides motivation for people to feel better and better about themselves. Think of self-esteem as a "verb" or action condition, leading to self-confidence, which is a "noun" or final condition.

Self-esteem then should be constant, not subject to the lows of your last defeat or the highs of your last victory. You're good at some things, not so good at others; in fact, you may be better at some things at certain times and not other times.

You can see the somewhat nauseating effect on self-esteem if you "ride the waves" in the upper graphic shown below, and are constantly affected by external events and feedback. When you are sure about who you are and maintain your self-worth through the heady "wins" and the brickbat thrown at your head during "losses," you possess what I call "self-mastery."

Self-esteem as a roller coaster

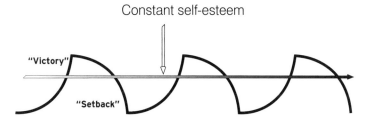

Self-esteem in two scenarios

Self-mastery tends to immunize you against invidious unsolicited feed-back, and protect you from doubt after defeats. It provides you with resilience.

One more, important point about self-esteem, resilience, and Thriving. If you believe your locus of learning is *external*—that is, you continue to learn from outside influences which you choose (the antithesis of unsolicited feedback)—you are resilient even in "defeat." This is due to the belief system which tells you that you can always "go outside" and learn more to overcome the setback and Thrive in the future. It keeps the cycle going depicted in the second graphic above.

However, if you believe that you already know all you need to know and that your learning is complete, then your cycle ends with each defeat, since you've "shot your bolt."[52] Since you have no more skills or tools, and nothing left to learn or acquire (and you may have lost the capacity to do so), you become depressed and withdrawn. We see this all the time on the job, and in many cases in personal relation-ships. (Just watch people who fanatically resist counseling, or business people who don't want coaching.)

Talent outs when you acquire the talent and allow it to take shape and grow. That occurs in businesses with employees, and it occurs with you and your attitude.

We need to constantly challenge the "victimology" mindset and poverty mentality that tends to engulf us in the perceived misery of others, and avoid becoming enablers and commiseraters. When we avoid being victimized ourselves, we rise above the fray. You're not "oppressing" anyone if you fail to feed their victim hunger, but if you are nonetheless perceived that way, no worries.

---

[52] A term from the old crossbowmen, who took about a minute to rewind their firing mechanism after each short arrow—bolt—was discharged. Once you shot your bolt you were defenseless in the interim before the next one.

It's better to be an oppressor than a victim in a world where victims feel they are entitled to what everyone else has, regardless of talent, and where "oppressors" are those who gain through talent, ability, and self-esteem, which always "out" in the end.

CHAPTER 8

If you don't blow your own horn, there is no music

Learning to be your own symphony

There is such a phenomenon as "healthy selfishness." Ayn Rand pretty much covers the waterfront on the issue.[53] Who is John Galt?!

The most powerful catalyst to helping others is to help yourself. That doesn't mean that you take the lion's share[54] of the meal or to break in line at the theater, as tempting as the latter may be. It means that it's tough to donate to a charity if you have no money, difficult to coach a youth team when you have no time, and impossible to take care of infirm family members when you, yourself, are bedridden.

You can't be ashamed to blow your own horn, no matter what key, what tune, or what volume. If you don't blow it, there is no music that is distinctly you.

If you really had priapism, would your first stop *really* be a doctor?

I adore the warning that attends Cialis® and Viagra® "penile erection dysfunction" medications. Among them is the admonition that if your erection lasts for more than four hours (a condition known as "priapism"), you should immediately consult a doctor.

---

[53] See *Atlas Shrugged* as the canonical story of never debasing one's own talent. Originally printed by Random House in 1957, there are scores of reissues today.

[54] Bear in mind this phrase has been corrupted, and originally meant "to take everything."

Now, I don't know about other males reading this, and a four-hour erection might engender many things, but rushing to the emergency room isn't one of them. In fact, it doesn't rate in my top 50.

We beat ourselves to death when we are down, but seldom scream with exultation when we're up (no pun intended). We may or may not bemoan our dire fates, either suffering in silence or rending our garments and engaging in lamentation publicly. But we seldom exalt with gusto. We feel it may be boastful or braggadocio.

Various cultures actively thwart anyone trying to stand out in a crowd, and you may be surprised by some of them. In Australia, as I note elsewhere, there is the "tall poppy syndrome," meaning the tall flower, more successful than others and obviously so, is the one that gets clipped. In pragmatic terms, this translates as follows: If you attempt to (or inadvertently) stand out in a crowd, the egalitarian blade will cut you back down to size. School phrases such as "teacher's pet" and business slurs such as "suck up" are the edge of the blade.

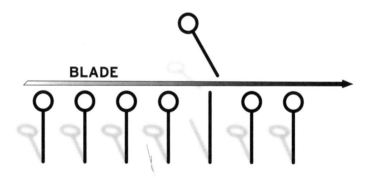

The tall poppy gets whacked

The way to balance your life is to recognize your victories along with your setbacks. To ignore the former while wallowing in the latter is an exercise in martyrdom, and we've already established that you can easily grow to love that work.

This means that you can spend a lifetime trying to correct things that aren't as good as others and *never grow or live much of a life*. That's because you're creating criteria that have nothing to do with your own success, only others' existence (and, perhaps, not even their success).

There's a reason that people hand out cigars when a baby is born, whip out photos of grandchildren, and carry clippings of a niece's scholarship announcement: They want to continue to relive the moment, the joy, the adrenaline rush, the excitement. They are engaged in innocent bragging (everyone whips out photos, Pavlovian in its occurrence, and you might as well order lunch).

However, most of these interactions are really about *others*, not about us. We readily tell someone about our bum knee or auto accident, but we don't proclaim that we received a promotion or had an article published or bought a new car.

We don't feel it's "proper," and we know too many braggarts who have spent their lives boring us to tears. But those braggarts aren't us. We need to extend our periods of happiness, no less than the grandchild's birth or the class valedictorian award.

We don't do enough to proclaim and therefore prolong our own victories and elation.

There is a difference between one-upsmanship and honestly stating your successes. Everything is about motive and context. If someone says that they're just back from Paris and loved the Intercontinental Hotel, you don't say, "What? We only stay at the Georges Cinq!" But if someone says to you, "How was your trip to Paris," responding that you had a lovely suite at the Georges Cinq with three bathrooms, two grand pianos and a butler is a perfectly fine response, especially with a smile on your face. If the other person is sincere and secure, he or she will say, "Wow, tell me how you did that!"

If they are not sincere and secure, what do you care how they feel? No, I'm serious. You can't live your life by daintily stepping around the eggshells of others' inadequacies. There is an infinite number of eggshells, and you have to get moving.

I had a consulting and coaching client for several years who was the CEO of a large insurance company. I had never mentioned to him that I am (ahem) an award-winning professional speaker, as well, and a member of the Professional Speakers Hall of Fame®.

One day he approached me to help him find a keynote speaker for a major insurance industry event with 250 CEOs in the audience. He was the program chair. And I had a terribly tough time convincing him I was, indeed, the person he needed, and not just a consultant trying to horn in on a gig I didn't deserve! The event was a huge success, and I did him a substantial favor, so it was win/win/win. But it came close to nothing/nothing/nothing. I hadn't played the right music prior to the request.

As an individual, you have unique strengths, experiences, and perspective. It doesn't matter where you went to school (or *if* you went to school), what your gender is, how old you are, what your background consists of, or your physiognomy. All of us get to contribute what we are and who we are. But we can't do that, ironically, if we choose not to provide it. We are our own worst governor.

I was talking to a group about creating one's "story of life" and a woman remarked that her life was boring.

"What did you do after high school?" I asked.

"That's the thing, I went into the army."

" *Where?"*

"West Point."

"You must have been in one of the first classes accepting women."

"I was in *the* first class with women."

"Did you make it through? At what rank?"

"I became the captain of cadets."

"You were the top cadet in the class?"

"Yes. But then I just went into the service."

"What branch?"

"I became a paratrooper...."

You get the idea. This happens repeatedly when I coach and counsel people. They feel their own stories and experiences are lackluster and/ or shouldn't be discussed. I find them fascinating and sometimes mesmerizing.

I'm here to tell you that no one is lackluster and every story should be discussed, especially the victories, successes, and achievements. If you don't blow your own horn, there is no music that is uniquely yours. And that means you're forever dancing to someone else's tune and tempo.

When you have something good going, talk about it, scream about it, roll around in it. It will continue to nourish you when times are tough, and the momentum will carry you through to the next success. Have you ever seen a dog find a great smell and proceed to rub around in it, as if applying *eau de canine*?

That's how we should roll around in our success, barking and howling in pleasure!

If you can do it, it ain't braggin'

Baseball pitcher Dizzy Dean's famous aphorism just happens to be one of those immutable laws of the universe. I've always preached the following definitions:

- **Confidence**: The honest-to-goodness belief that you can help others to learn and grow through your talent.

- **Arrogance**: The honest-to-goodness belief that you can help others through your talent, but you have nothing left to learn yourself.

- **Smugness**: Arrogance without the talent.

There is an admittedly thin line between confidence and arrogance, and I deliberately skate on it. But in order to Thrive, you're better off being supremely confident and infrequently arrogant (when you lean too far over the line) than you are being humble because you're afraid to go near the line.

One of the things we quickly learn in business is that confident, powerful people love to have powerful, competent people around them. They do *not* enjoy "yes men."[55] Hence, salespeople shouldn't appear as "venders" but rather as peers, well-dressed, well-spoken, and well-read. The old bromides about "dressing down" and "dumbing down" to your audience so that the other party feels elevated are simply relics of the past.

Weak people employ and prefer weak people around them. The nastiest, most profane CEO I ever met had a roomful of pathetic lieutenants around him. Who else would accept that kind of treatment except an inferior?

---

[55] My apologies to the gender police, but "yes people" doesn't capture the obsequious nature of the intent for me, and sounds more like a motivational singing group.

The same dynamics apply to our lives.

I'm suspicious of a ski instructor who sits in the lodge slurping brandy and gives me "advice" on how to ski the next morning. I'll happily pay for the instructor who goes up the lift with me, says, "Do what I do," and whose posterior I observe in front of me as I traverse and descend the mountain. I want that kind of confidence and competence demonstrated for me.

If you demonstrate you can do it, people will follow you, and if you fail in the attempt, they will identify with you.

Ironically, you Thrive by demonstrating you are Thriving. All of us have myriad talents, some mainstream, some not. It's the visible application of those talents which creates a full and enviable life.

Being proud of real accomplishment is an essential trait which too many people abjure because they believe it to be bragging, even though they can do it. If someone asks you to play the piano, and you can do so, do it. If you're asked to provide insights on a vacation spot, provide them. If you can deliver the speech to the civic group on behalf of your fundraiser, then stand up.

No one has ever been able to Thrive by avoiding the nourishment of the sunlight, the fresh air, and the new experience. You can't Thrive hiding in the shadows because you're afraid someone might consider you "bold" or "assertive" or "overly confident."

People who are self-absorbed insist on their personal pleasure and comfort trumping everyone else's. But those who are highly confident are able to establish consensus, make intelligent compromises, and influence others—which ultimately lead to personal objectives being met and great happiness.

There is a psychological phenomenon known as "projection," which is the extension of one's personal traits to others, without reason. For example, if I had a tough time learning to speak Spanish and I was told that you were undertaking it, projection would prompt me to say, "The irregular verbs are terrible and the speed of comprehension very difficult, so don't plan to be able to speak socially for at least six months."

The issue in that exchange is that I assume you're no better at this than I am, and should you master the language in a short time, I'd be threatened by my perceived weakness or lack of affinity (or I'd tell people that you had probably studied it in school and didn't revel in it). Of course, if I'm psychologically healthy, I'm going to say, "Here's what I had trouble with, I'll be interested to see if you manage it better and faster and, if so, perhaps you can give me some pointers."

If I can do it, it ain't braggin', and if *you* can do it, it ain't braggin', either!

People who moan, "I wish I had played the piano when I was asked," or "I wish I had volunteered to make the presentation," are, ironically, people who could have played the piano and made the presentation. We're not talking about skills deficiencies but rather about volitional deficiencies. The good news is that we can change those deficits ourselves, once we recognize what we're doing to ourselves: ***Wishing our lives away.***

Dwight Eisenhower aspired to retire as a full colonel, having never commanded troops in World War I. He became a very good staff officer and then, through history and happenstance, went from colonel to five-star general in just over two years at the start of World War II. He never did command troops until the North Africa campaign, which had its share of misadventures and errors, but prepared Ike for Normandy and hero status, and the Presidency.

If you *think* you can do it, it ain't braggin', either.

Merely stand your ground and you'll stand out in a crowd

"Putting a stake in the ground" comes from the ancient Aztec warriors, as we described earlier. These days you can stand out in a crowd without taking bizarre, flamboyant, or dramatic actions. In an age when our schools are seeking equality and not excellence, and people seek not just an equal starting line but also an equal finish line, talented and confident people will stand out as the crowd around them ebbs.

It's sort of like being an anchored boat while the other craft are all washed out to sea by the departing tide.

That anchor is a combination of your talent and your willingness to apply it. That is, the anchor isn't sufficient in and of itself. It has to be cast overboard and obtain purchase. The anchor is your stake. It does no good on the boat.

We are faced today with people who cannot use language correctly, cannot find China on a map (much less Bolivia), and don't know the years of the First World War. Kelly Pickler, a finalist on *American Idol* some years back, appeared on the television quiz show, *Are You Smarter Than a Fifth Grader* (she apparently is not) and informed the audience that she thought Europe was a country and had never heard of Hungary. Miss Teen USA from South Carolina in 2007 made YouTube history by rambling for 48 seconds in pure nonsense during her interview competition.

Television anchors routinely say "between you and I" as if to sound elegant, and just this morning I heard a radio newscaster comment that a philanthropist "bidded" on a piece of art at auction.

Here's a test which you can complete in the privacy of your room, airplane seat, or park bench. If you read the papers and are cognizant of the world around you, you can stand out in any crowd, much less a receding one. Scoring appears in a box on the following page:

Common Knowledge Test

1. What is the correct chronology, earliest to latest, of these events?
   ❑ Civil War   ❑ Mexican War   ❑ Spanish American War

2. NASA is an acronym for what?

3. East Pakistan declared its independence from Pakistan and became what country?

4. Which of these words is not a preposition?
   ❑ among   ❑ with   ❑ but   ❑ between

5. What author wrote *The Other Side of Paradise, The Great Gatsby,* and *The Last Tycoon?*

6. A triangle with two equal sides is known as what?

7. *Ode to Joy* and *The Fifth Symphony* were written by what composer?

8. What is known colloquially as "The Great White Way"?

9. What is the counterpart of the equinox?

10. What does GMT stand for in relation to the longitude for establishing time?

Most people, when confronted with a troubling or complicated situation, tend to float to the rear. You can spot them: They lose eye contact, don't volunteer, pretend to be engaged in something else. Their "presence" has diminished, their spirit has ebbed. *Merely by establishing eye contact, providing positive non-verbal behavior (smiling, nodding, gesturing), and taking part in the discussion, you establish yourself as valuable and valued.*

That's right, Thriving is about simply staying in the game. This isn't a contest that can knock you out, though it is one in which you can knock yourself out if you choose to retire.

"Why didn't I say something? I knew the answer!" moans the wishers. "Next time I'm going to say something," vows the survivor. "I didn't want to take the risk," justifies the fearful.

Thriving is about trying. If you're not failing, you're not trying! Here are some examples:

- Throughout history, from the Tyrannosaurus[56] to the cheetah, predators have been successful only about 10 percent of the time. That's right, it takes 10 attempts to feed the family.

- Abraham Lincoln lost elections readily, lost debates regularly, and was considered "washed up" when he launched his successful Presidential bid.

- Most of Edison's inventions and patents were never developed into commercially viable products.

- Steve Jobs is responsible for the iPhone, et. al., but he was also responsible for the dud called "Lisa." (You don't recall? Well, that's my point.)

- My bestseller, *Million Dollar Consulting*, was rejected by 15 publishers before it was accepted for publication. It's now in its fourth edition, over 18 consecutive years.

---

[56] The T Rex dominated the land for roughly 90 million years. By the way, we've been here for maybe 10,000. That should prevent all of us from developing too much of a superiority complex.

If you're not failing, you're just not trying, and those who claim they've never failed fall into one or more of these three categories:

1. They are lying.

2. They've never tried anything innovative or important.

3. They've failed and don't know it.

Answers and Scoring for the General Knowledge Test

1. Mexican War, Civil War, Spanish American War, in that order.

2. National Aeronautics and Space Administration.

3. Bangladesh.

4. But (it's a conjunction).

5. F. Scott Fitzgerald.

6. Isosceles.

7. Beethoven.

8. Broadway in New York (because of all the neon lights).

9. The solstice.

10. Greenwich Mean Time.

Scoring:

10: Dramatically well-informed.

7-9: Decently well-informed.

4-6: Relatively uninformed.

1-3: Uninformed.

0: Comatose.

Standing your ground can do a lot for you these days. Now, unlike my wonderment about the Aztecs not advancing, let's find out how you can become more offensive, in the best possible sense!

The two-word propellant ("Of course!")

If you want to start Thriving, start saying "Of course." When clients ask me if I can do something which (I know and they don't know) I've never done before, I say, "Of course!" When reporters ask if I can comment on a particular incident for their publication, "Of course!" When someone says, "Would you like to take over the fundraising committee?" I say, "Of course NOT!" (Okay, that was a test.)

My point is that we spend too much time bobbing and weaving, suspicious that the client has devious motives, or the great price must mean inferior merchandise, or the opportunity also presents tremendous risk. So by the time we analyze, parse, dissect, evaluate, assess, and use a food taster, the opportunity is gone and we're saying, "I wish I would have...." and we're once again wishing our lives away.

My biography, website, blog, Twitter home page, and sandwich sign board record the quote from *The New York Post* that I am "...one of the most highly respected independent consultants in the country." That came about when a reporter found one of my listings and asked if he could interview me on the management techniques used by the first winner of the *Survivor* reality show, Richard Hatch (subsequently jailed on tax evasion charges, showing that he's not such a great survivor). I said, "Of course," and we set a date.

Of course, I had never, ever watched the program.

So, I called my daughter, an executive producer at MTV in New York, and told her to get all the past tapes and all the sushi she could carry and meet me at The Peninsula Hotel in New York. As we seriously raised our sodium and mercury levels, she explained the show and I saw Hatch, sure enough, use a half-dozen common manipulative tactics (e.g., "let's you and him fight").

When the reporter interviewed me later that week I had my sound bites ready, and in a front page of the Sunday feature section, I was the only interviewee in a 100-column-inch lead story. And I was introduced as, guess what, "...one of the most highly respected independent consultants in the country."

I'm not advocating that you agree to just anything, which is why the fundraising committee is out. But I am telling you that we're here to take prudent risk, not strive for zero risk. The biggest bruise in a fall is usually to your ego, which is marvelously self-healing if you allow it to be.

I repeat: *We're not here to stick our toes in the water. We're here to make waves. The water doesn't care. You should.*

Not everyone has a hidden agenda. You can't look at a banana as a potentially slippery weapon once the peel is removed, the banana eaten, and the peel carelessly discarded in your path. That's not prudence, it's paranoia. A banana is a fruit, not a land mine.

Yet we go through life on the alert for everything that may harm us, including opportunities, gift horses, and manna from heaven. Henry James observed that "Life is a slow, reluctant march into enemy territory." But Elton Trueblood viewed it differently: "Faith is not a blind leap into nothing but a thoughtful walk in the light we have."

James was talking of the clock running down, and his novels often reflect a basic fatalism. Dr. Trueblood was a Quaker who devoted his life to public service. They both need to be read, in my opinion, but which course should one lead is my question.

We had a terrier once named Phoebe. One day, for no reason, Phoebe decided she would not turn a sharp corner in the upper hallway. One of us would have to be there to assure her it was okay, and only then would she turn the corner to trot on down to the bedroom. We finally broke her of the habit, and she (and we) were all the better for it.

Are you afraid to look around the corner? This isn't a battle where you'll get whacked for sticking your neck out. Are you stalling in the hallway, waiting for others to assure you that there's nothing there? The others may not be available, they may also be scared, they may lie to you. Isn't it better to look for yourself?

After all, how bad can it be just to take a look? If you see a larger dog there, you can still hold your ground or retreat. But the probability is that all you're going to see is a route leading to another destination.

If you want to Thrive—right now, today, this lifetime—then you have to start saying "Of course!" to life. (There is a song we sing in church in which the refrain goes, "I say YES, my Lord!" which is a constant affirmation of one's faith.)

The people who are offered and steadfastly refuse a new kind of food, and who have no allergy or physical reason for not sampling it, reveal to me a fundamental flaw about their entire view of life. When someone offers a taste, why wouldn't you say, "Of course!" Doesn't it make sense to test a small sampling to see if it is pleasing? Or is the adamantine refusal to try what you've never experienced indicative of a very controlled, cautious, and pessimistic life?

Absent a rare allergy, can an ounce of lobster, or grits, or poi, or clams, or linguini puttanesca really damage you? What about trying the theater, or ballet, or snorkeling, or writing an essay, or watching public television? Can this stuff really harm you? Is a steadfast refusal to say "Of course I'll try it" really an essential Jesuitical position which must be maintained to keep the faith? (Just today I heard someone at the gym say, "I'd *never* attend a play!" Is this the kind of attitude that will improve your fitness, physical or otherwise?)

As noted, there are limits. You perhaps don't say "Of course!" to skydiving, or ultimate cage fighting, or pornography or buying land in Florida during an infomercial. I'm not advocating blind faith, but I am supporting *faith in your judgment in a larger dimension than probably exists today.*

You have to say "Of course!" to life. After that, you need to rely on the positive consequence of accepting more and more challenge, diversity, and prudent risk. Visiting a casino to try to win money to pay your bills is not prudent risk, it's stupid. But avoiding making a speech to your colleagues because you might be embarrassed isn't avoiding prudent risk, it's overly frightened behavior. Your credit rating requires a lot more care and protection than does your ego.

The way to avoid wishing your life away and pining about lost opportunities is to listen to your child asking you to throw a ball; watching your dog imploring you to take him for a ride; considering if you should take a vacation on impulse; analyzing whether to accept the high-profile project at work; thinking about learning to play an instrument; and considering patching up that relationship which used to be so strong and now is so painful.

And then saying, "Of course!"

Speak now, never hold your peace

I've never understood the "speak now or forever hold your peace" in traditional marriage ceremonies. Does that mean that, if you find out two days later that the groom is a serial murderer, you don't inform the bride because you missed the chance? (With 41 percent of all marriages currently ending in divorce, I'd think you'd want to know well ahead of this point, but that's another story in another book.)

One of *the* greatest causes of "I wish I had...." is in not speaking up whenever the spirit moves you. There are all those bromides, I know, about keeping your mouth shut, and once you say something you can never take it back.

But you know what? When the judge says to the jury, "You will disregard that last remark," the bell can't be unrung, and somehow the jury is smart enough to figure it out more often than not. A great deal more damage has been done when witnesses refuse to divulge details or the defendant is afraid of incriminating someone else.

You can't take back what was said, but if it was wrong or damaging, you can apologize and atone. It happens all the time. Economic forecasters are notoriously off the mark, yet they're paid to do it all again next year. If they were paid like ball players, they'd all be in the minors. (If they had the accuracy of bookies, we'd all get rich in the stock market.) Aren't you better off when someone tells you that you have a head of lettuce caught in your incisors, so that you don't hop into the next meeting looking like a rabbit?

In an age of instant communication, "reply all" on emails, and cell phones in everyone's pocket (or protruding like alien life forms from their ears), we are remarkably reticent about voicing our ideas, objections, support, and/or perplexity. And the more you stifle what you have to say, the more the frustration builds. *You don't Thrive by choking down sentiments any more than you enjoy a good dinner by choking down the steak.*

When I consulted with Hewlett-Packard, a great company, I was dumbfounded by the "pre-meeting meetings" that occurred between small groups of people who didn't want to threaten consensus by speaking out at the scheduled meeting. This created a huge amount of lost time and extra cost, not to mention consensus at the price of effectiveness.

Your attitude must be that you are doing service to others by speaking out, and you must overcome the fear of being seen as:

- divisive
- tactless
- presumptuous
- outspoken
- provocative
- pretentious
- contrarian
- arrogant
- preposterous

(Sort of reads like one of my performance evaluations back at Prudential!)

What's the worst that can happen? So long as your *motivation* is to help others and not to manipulate, delay, or undermine, then your approach is pure. If you manage to help people with ideas they hadn't considered or risks they hadn't anticipated, or opportunities they hadn't exploited, that's great. If you delay the decision by an hour or a day, so what?

And, worst case, if you offend someone or are in error with your facts, then you apologize and get on with your life.

The Greeks believed that it was glorious to die in battle (go Spartans!), and so they fought to the death, even against overwhelming odds. The Romans believed that your strategy should be to win the war and not merely the current battle, and it was fine to retreat to fight again another day. I'm a Roman in that regard. Apologize and return. It's crazy to defend something that is wrong.

But you have to be on the battlefield in either case, armed and ready. That may be a tad hyperbolic, but you get the drift: You're not in the game if you're not willing to speak out. If you never speak unless you are assured of accuracy and a warm reception, then you will never speak.

We have an obligation to help others by speaking out in truth, not by shielding them with perfidious silence.

Confederate General James Longstreet tried to stop Pickett's ill-conceived charge, but was afraid to oppose Robert E. Lee too strongly. I once met one of the NASA engineers who argued that the O-rings were inadequate just prior to the Challenger disaster, but his superiors would not raise the issue further up the ladder. I've seen children get into trouble with cheating, drugs, alcohol, and abuse, because their parents and counselors didn't want to confront or use "discipline."

The government currently beseeches people to speak out if they see anything remotely suspicious in public areas or while traveling. It's interesting that they would have to make a point of what would seem to be an obvious response. What's the worst thing that can happen? The cops come and take away someone's luggage or blow up a bag with groceries in it? But what's the best that can happen? Lives could have been saved.

Our need to speak out is vital for society, but even more important for our individual well being. Artificially and unilaterally subordinating your feelings, sentiments, and experiences is unhealthy and stressful. The stress is a double-whammy: We're conflicted in the moment as to whether to speak, and when we don't we suffer the "I wish I had...." syndrome many times later on.

The great wit and observer of the human condition, Le Duc de la Rochefoucauld, wrote that "Few men are wise enough to prefer useful criticism to treacherous praise." We need to give people the chance by offering useful criticism, feedback, observations, and conclusions.

This needn't be in the form of unsolicited feedback, which is a phenomenon that is almost always conducted for the sender, not the receiver. I'm speaking of "solicited feedback," such as occurs in public meetings, family discussions, business debates, and other forums where everyone, ostensibly, is airing issues in order to hear from others. There's a big difference between telling your neighbor over coffee, "Oh, I meant to tell you that that jacket makes you look fat," and replying *when asked* if you like the jacket, "It's nice material, but I don't think it fits you well."

You may think "potato/potahto" about all this, but I don't think so. Speaking out helps you Thrive by helping others to Thrive. At those times when others are expecting opinion and commentary, it's criminal (and certainly unfriendly in the truest sense) to withhold information that may assuage pain, or prevent embarrassment, or improve someone's condition. The ultimate act of selfishness is believing that your words always have to be received cordially and your opinions always have to be regarded as holy writ and agreed upon.

You don't "hold" your peace. You provide peace for others through honest discourse, and you provide peace for yourself through speaking up and allowing yourself to Thrive.

You have to speak out in order to stand out.

CHAPTER 9!

The five traits of the masters of their fates

You are not what you eat

The opposite of victimology is self-mastery, which I'll define here as the ability to make autonomous decisions, evaluate their results, and create direction for further improvement and fulfillment. It is also the ability to apply one's talents and derive an effective "effort/reward" correlation, so that the gratification for exercising talents exceeds the work on creating and applying them.

This is far from an ideal world, but at least it should be *your world*.

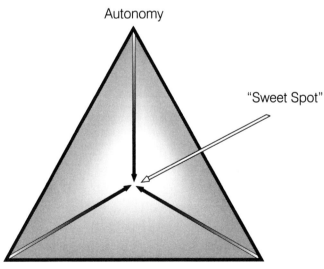

Autonomy

"Sweet Spot"

Application of Talents

Appropriate Reward Correlation

Trait 1
Resilience: The lessons of the ice plant

When we lived in Redwood Shores, outside of San Francisco, we had been married for 15 years, had two small children, and didn't realize that we had not yet conquered the world. California has a way of changing all that.

On the perimeter of our ranch home and it's half-acre lot, there was a West Coast beast known as ice plant. It grew along the ground in a vine-like fashion, became quite thick, and overcame any resistance it met, from wildflowers to old fences. Within its serpentine depths lives snails, slugs, and all kinds of nocturnal critters perfectly safe from their predators.

I decided that the constantly–advancing, somewhat menacing ice plant had to go, and gathered clippers, snippers, pruners, hatchets, and all kinds of things short of napalm. Half the time, I was unsuccessful in making a dent—there were layers of the stuff. And the other half, what was cut grew back within a week at twice the density.

I gave up, stored the tools, and learned that ice plant stops itself when it becomes so thick the underlying layers die, or the distance is too great from its nutrients. (It could only transgress on so much pavement.) In addition, the town would come by once a year with gruesome machinery and knock it back a couple of feet.[57]

We all need that kind of resilience, because the world is doing a lot to cut us back and knock us down.

Resilience means that you do not require the support or input of others to sustain yourself. You may have affiliation needs, you may enjoy working with or leading others, you may prefer social events over individual interests. This is not to say you shouldn't be an extrovert or outgoing personality.

---

[57] I'm sure today California has a Preserve Ethical Treatment for Ice Plant Association of some kind.

But it does mean that you are capable, when necessary, of working independently and listening only to your own judgment. True resilience does not require the validation of others. It doesn't mean that you're always "up" and that you won't ever be down. But it does mean that you rebound relatively quickly and don't suffer lasting adverse effects of defeats and setbacks.

Your resilience on the chart on page 171 is near the middle—the "sweet spot." Here are the hallmarks of resilient people:

Alan's Resilience Factors

- Resilient people have a profound sense of right and wrong without needing others to vindicate or verify their actions.

- They do not overreact to success or failure, but keep events in perspective.

- They will take prudent risk and be prepared to change course or correct inappropriate directions.

- They do not choose consensus as a formal or informal leadership style (they either make the decision or allow others to, but they don't try to create temporary agreement).

- They do not mope, feel guilty, need to "recharge their batteries," or vacillate. (They make decisions and do not second-guess themselves.)

- They find happiness, positives, and the upbeat in circumstances and conditions where most don't.

- They forgive themselves when they've erred, and think of themselves as good people.

Resilience is not a competency, it's a behavior. You must become predisposed to be resilient through adoption of the right belief system and consequent attitudes.

Here's how you can change your behaviors to be more resilient:

- Reduce your dependence on others to assess your actions and "pass judgment."

- When you do seek feedback, accept it only from trusted others whom you choose; never accept unsolicited feedback.

- Understand and embrace your true strengths, assets, and contributions. Rely on these—not the last success or setback—to guide your actions.

- Accept the wisdom of making decisions that can be corrected and adjusted, and alleviate yourself of the pressure of having to somehow make the "right" decision in advance, every time.

- Remember that your life is about success, not perfection.

Trait 2
Eternal learning: "It's not a problem" IS a problem

The words "you're welcome" have largely disappeared from the English vernacular. We are usually subjected today, in response to a "thank you," to "not a problem," or the shorter form, "no problem." (In Australia, it's predominantly "no worries.")

People to whom we are expressing our gratitude—wait staff, gas station attendants, emergency medical technicians, librarians—had almost overnight decided that the proper response to being thanked is to reassure the obligated person that they were not unduly discomfited in providing the service. Presumably, if it *were* a problem, then our steak wouldn't have arrived on time, the gas wouldn't have been pumped, the book wouldn't have been found, and our heart would not have been defibrillated.

Not to worry, but I have a problem with that.

A fundamental trait of masters of their fate is eternal learning. That means you never "dumb down" your abilities, competencies, or brilliance. The idiotic rubric that we should "dress down" and "dumb down" to our clients' level is crass nonsense created by those who have no self-esteem themselves. They are intimidated by clients and unsure as to what standards they should adhere.

They don't learn, they flee to what they perceive is safe (and low) ground.

Eternal learning means that you're constantly surprised by how stupid you were two weeks ago. If you can accept that and understand that it is part of true growth and mastery, then you'll be a natural lifelong learner. But most aren't.

I remember talking to a colleague who, like me, had been in the consulting and speaking professions for a long time. We were sharing our mutual wonder at how much more we knew about our craft today than when we began.

"Sometimes," my colleague confided, "I just want to call all my old clients and say, 'I'm sorry, I'm sorry, I didn't know then what I know now, and I need to give you your money back'!" I knew exactly how he felt (though I would not have opted for that particular remedy!).

I've continued to watch manners and class decline, and "not a problem" is a metaphor for the deterioration of norms. We've become a much more informal society, which in and of itself is not a crime,[58] but we've also become a society where higher standards and informed behavior are no longer observed nor even appreciated.

Eternal learning also entails never forgetting the right stuff. Here are some examples that tell me instantly whether the person with whom

---

[58] Although when running outfits become the default attire, and people wear tee-shirts, shorts, and flip-flops in church, I'd maintain that informality has become sloth and disrespect.

I'm dealing is educated, aware, and sophisticated. With a partner, colleague, friend, or just trusted other, it's rather important:

- **The way you hold your knife, the way you sip your tea.** You can use your cutlery in the continental style or American style, both are correct, but the Paleolithic style is not. Stabbing meat and holding a knife like a dagger are something out of Macbeth. (Your bread dish is *always* to your left, your glassware to your right.)

- **Speak to me only with thine eyes.** If you're talking with food in your mouth you're a troglodyte. No one else should get to see what you're trying to digest.

- **Talk to me.** But only with the right grammar. "Between you and I" is an incorrect, effete attempt to sound better than your knowledge permits. The speaker implies, the listener infers. They are not synonyms. Prone is on your stomach, supine is on your back. I could go on. Those who try to minimize these real distinctions and nuance in the language would prefer that we all, well, dumb down because it's too much effort to try to learn.

- **Are you looking at me?** Unless you have terminally low self-esteem, you'll have to accept that we all age. There is nothing wrong with taking cosmetic actions to improve appearance, but no man looks natural with chestnut dyed hair, and women over a certain size shouldn't wear clothing with writing across the derriere (some of them manage, and have the room, to fit entire sentences).

- **Where are your manners?** One should return phone calls and email promptly; "thank you" notes remain appropriate in response to a gift or favor; announcing who you are when you call is proper; as requested, respond quickly to RSVP notes; and stop flossing in public.

I know that these "rules" can seem pedestrian and unimportant (or perhaps "aristocratic" in an egalitarian-crazed society). But self-mastery is about accepting and conforming to certain standards. People no longer wear shirts and ties to fly on airplanes (as was the norm in the late 50s and early 60s), but you should refrain from shouting on your cell phone, allowing your kids to run down the aisles, and getting drunk. I've been in airline clubs, once restricted to invitation only but "democratized" after lawsuits from those who demanded entry, where some bozo in shorts and sandals has his feet up on a table and is cutting his toe nails.

Is that really progress?

People who are masters of their fate learn continually, both to improve and to reinforce and retain those practices and traits that serve us all the best. We can't merely become better and better at what we're already good at. We have to raise the bar and aspire to higher standards—which often includes resisting the breakdown of old standards.

Truth: "I'm constantly surprised by how stupid I was two weeks ago," but I'm happily content that I can accept that and continue to integrate the best that already exists and the best that I encounter coming down the pike. Sometimes you stand alone in doing so, but the rewards are well worth it in terms of mastering your fate.

Believe me, that's not a problem.

Trait 3
Self-esteem: "Follow me!"

When I first began counseling consultants in the early 90s, I was convinced that the major problem for any entrepreneur was a lack of sufficient capitalization. I was positive, and wrote about it.

I was wrong. (See: I'm constantly surprised by how stupid I was two weeks ago.)

The major obstacle then and now is a profound lack of self-esteem. If you want to Thrive, you need to feel good about yourself, irrespective of whether you're currently experiencing success in the endeavor in front of your nose. As I've mentioned, I can't play any musical instrument, not even the radio, very well, yet I nonetheless feel good about myself. I've seen a lot of great musicians who don't feel good about themselves. They may be able to play music, but can't blow their own horn.

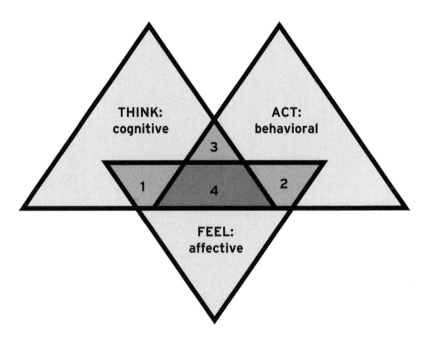

1. Totally internal, no manifestation
2. Acting viscerally, not with forethought
3. Responding to analysis, no passion
4. Totally engaged

In the figure on the previous page you see the classical "think, act, feel" factors. All three are required for healthy self-esteem.

- If you *think* about an issue and *feel* its impact, yet take no action, you are totally internally engaged. There is no manifestation in the environment. No one truly understands how you think and feel, and you may well receive either no respect or simply be ignored.

- If you solely *feel* emotions and viscerally *act* on them, you are rash and impulsive, with little or no forethought. You won't be regarded as reliable in a crisis, and may well be seen as a "hothead."

- If you merely *think* and *act* while divorced emotionally, you'll be seen as passionless, an umpire of the game others are playing, cold and uninvolved with no stake in the action, no skin in the game.

- You are only totally engaged when you are involving your *thinking* and *feeling* and taking consequent *action*. Then you tend to act appropriately for the occasion, with due moderation or outrage, but always as a symbol of reason and passion appropriately and effectively combined.

People with high self-esteem are not reliant on that last piece of unsolicited feedback, the shrug or moan into which Gnostic meaning is divined. They have appropriate expectations of themselves and others, which means they are far less likely to be surprised, disappointed, and ineffectual in interpersonal dealings and relationships. I want to return to Bandura for our purposes here.

In the next chart you can see that high efficacy beliefs and high expectations create engagement and satisfaction, another way to look at the "sweet spot" at the beginning of this chapter. When efficacy is high but expectations low (e.g., your employer isn't calling upon your talents,

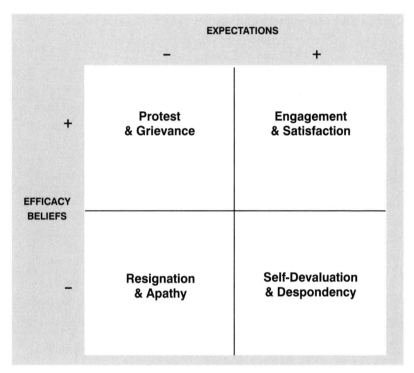

Expectations and Efficacy Beliefs[59]

or your soul mate doesn't believe you're dependable), the victimology results: protest and grievance.

Conversely, when expectations are high but self-worth low, despondency, lack of resilience, and devaluation arise. That's because we believe we can never measure up to what's expected (and why so many parents have sent so many kids to therapy 25 years later).

Of course, when both are low, we encounter resignation and apathy. One of the classifications of suicide is called "anomic," meaning that normal social, religious, and workplace institutions are not providing inclusion, integration, or even relief. (The Greek etymology means

---

[59] From Albert Bandura's book, *Self-Efficacy* (Macmillan, 1997).

"without law," and the term has been used by psychologists to denote a failure of normal institutions to set rules for living and conduct.)

People with high self-esteem shout at you, figuratively, to follow them. People with low self-esteem tend to drift into the shadows of daily intercourse.

No one Thrives in shadows.

Alan's Self-Esteem Builders:

- **Acquire and hone skills**. The more skills you have (professional, social, technical, interpersonal, and so forth) the better you perform. The better your perform, the more you develop a sense of self-worth, and the more prone you are to develop still more skills.

- **Apply positive self-talk**. Your language informs your behavior. If you believe you succeeded through luck but someone else succeeded through talent, you're subordinating yourself. Even a setback is cause to speak positively if it were in a good cause and/or provided learning.[60]

- **Walk with the lions**. Enter tough debates, take on "experts," question what you find to be suspicious. Don't simply accept an idea or principle because someone else is "smarter" or has more "credentials." Rocket scientists have blown up a lot of taxpayers' money.

- **Build on strengths**. Eternally correcting weaknesses is the growth equivalent of Zeno's Paradox: Make 50 percent progress toward your goal every day and you'll never reach it. People (and teams and organizations) grow by building on strengths. Identify yours and exploit them. (This is why point #1 is so important, since it adds strengths to your armamenture.)

---

[60] One of the finest, most readable books on the subject is Martin Seligman's *Learned Optimism* (Knopf Doubleday, 2006).

- **Articulate your values.** Be cognizant of what you stand for and be able to explain it to others. Know when to hold and when to fold. If you're clear on what's important to you, you'll be more assured when you feel the need to defend or move forward.

Here's Jefferson: " In matters of principle, stand like a rock; in matters of taste, swim with the current."

Think of *self-esteem* as a verb or action, moving toward a noun or condition called *self-confidence*.

Trait 4
Perseverance: You win some, you lose some, and some get rained out, but you have to suit up for them all

The fourth trait might best be called "hanging on." There is the famous tale of "Rudy" who was undersized and under-talented, but nonetheless gave his all for Notre Dame football. He was regularly smashed up on the practice squads, proudly sat on the bench, and never played a game, until the very last one he was eligible for, when the coach was prevailed upon to put him in a rout in the last minute. (It made for a great movie, at the conclusion of which many of the men in the audience had suspiciously itchy eyes as the ending welled.)

Rudy hung on and achieved his goal. He had no right to play football, or even be included on one of the premier teams in the country at the time. But, somehow, he managed it.

At this writing, some New Haven, CT, firefighters won a ruling on their appeal to the U.S. Supreme Court. They felt they were the victims of "reverse discrimination," a hard thing to prove, and the city and lower courts disagreed with them. But they prevailed in their ultimate appeal when most thought the odds were against them. Perhaps they were. So what?

Masters of their fates Thrive. And they do so because they are perseverant and resilient. Don't misunderstand: They don't throw "good money after bad," they don't pursue clearly lost causes, and they don't bang their heads repeatedly against a wall expecting differing results each time.

But they do—we do—hang in there so long as there is a reasonable chance of success, our passion maintains us, and our goal is just.

Grant drove the Army of the Potomac south, toward Richmond, after victory *and* defeat facing Robert E. Lee. He knew his goal, had resources, and was perseverant, whereas every prior Union general facing Lee went back north to lick his wounds after defeats.

Hewlett and Packard kept their focus working out of a garage until their instruments could be perfected and purchased. Tiger Woods keeps practicing his golf strokes, and acts as if the occasional poor shot is a personal shortcoming which will be overcome as soon as possible. The amateur U.S. hockey team had no business beating the Russian professional team in the Olympics.

People who Thrive persevere. They overcome bad news, bad outcomes, and bad luck. They overcome loss and sorrow.

When you are facing tough circumstances, you have only these positive options:

- **Fix**. If something has gone wrong and must be restored, then fix it quickly and expeditiously. That can be a machine, a process, or a relationship. Nothing that's important should remain "broken" in our lives. There is no such thing as a "necessary evil," though there are evils we create or choose to endure.

- **Improve**. There are conditions that are historically fine but no longer serve us well. We have changed, grown, matured. It's time to elevate or alter our prior conditions. That may mean buying better clothes, taking more personal time, or establishing new relationships.

- **Cope**. There are issues which can neither be fixed nor improved. We must cope with loss, death, and heartbreak. These are inevitable consequences of living. We can learn to cope by seeking the positive and memorable and extending those traits through our loss. We must also keep loss in perspective. The loss of a job or opportunity is in a different universe from the loss of a loved one. I know a counselor who was "devastated" because the school system assigned her to a different school after a dozen years. For healthy people, that should be easy to cope with. The exigencies of daily life shouldn't "devastate" you.

People who Thrive persevere, and people who persevere Thrive, whether you win, lose, or draw. But in the longer term, people who have decided to Thrive win more often than not.

Trait 5
Love: No one says, "For the 'like' of God...."

Let me define "love" as a "deep, emotional, and amorous affection." It's an emotion that demands a certain *lack* of restraint, a freeing, an exuberance, an abandonment of inhibition. You can love a mate, love to paint, love your work, love your dog, love yourself.

Masters of their fate feel free to love, and do so repeatedly and continually. They form deep relationships and involvements, whether formalized or not. Thriving is about loving life.

These phrases don't quite work as well as the originals:

- "Will you still like me tomorrow?" (The Shirelles)

- "Like me or leave me...."

- "Like is in the air...."

- "She's the like of my life...."

To Thrive you have to free yourself to love. Thriving means taking big bites, making waves, taking risks. You must have passion to engage in those behaviors, and love is the fuel of passion.

The uninhibited, unrestrained engagement in love provides for these abilities:

- **Personal intimacy**. You need someone who "has your back." We all require solicited, personal feedback to let us know when we should exploit the successes we're enjoying and cut our losses on the setbacks. We deserve perspective and debate about our performance, experiences, and dreams. Intimacy isn't possible without love. The ability to create and maintain healthy relationships is dependent on our ability to give of ourselves and have others give for us.

- **The dynamic of continuity.** We come from family and create family, either through reproduction or extended family.[61] That aspect of being a part of the past, present, and future concurrently is a huge factor in personal well being. (My daughter brought our grandchildren to my wife's mother's funeral so that the family could relish in the continuation of our lives together.)

- **A positive outlet for our energies, frustrations, emotions, and talents**. Hobbies, interests, pastimes, and pursuits can be indulged in with great success or failure, but with passion nonetheless. The artist who tosses the paints in anger, the

---

[61] Hate me for this if you must, but I have never understood couples who choose *not* to raise children because kids present an interference in their lives. I think that is the most self-indulgent, truly sad position that I've ever heard from people who have decided to spend their lives together.

fisherman who bemoans the big ones getting away, the collector with the eternally incomplete collection—they are all expressing energy and talent and vitiating stress.

- **Perspective in life**. Loved ones and loving relationships provide true sounding boards for the deal that got away, the failed test, the missed plane, the stubbed toe. If we successfully and unabashedly love, we can remind ourselves—or readily have others remind us—that our "defeats" are not really fatal and our setbacks never final. There is a proportionality that is always present which prevents overreaction.

- **Tough love**. People who love us will endure our wrath and risk our rage because they have our true self-interests in mind—and know that we have theirs in mind as well. We seldom receive accurate feedback because most feedback is tainted with the needs of the sender.[62] Tough love can help end addictions, eliminate terrible judgment, and overcome perceived disabilities.

People think that Frank Sinatra sang about love. He did only by focusing on its antithesis: loneliness. "The One That Got Away," "Make It One for My Baby," "Down Mexico Way," "'Twas on the Isle of Capri"—I could go on for pages through his discography. He sang about losing love and not being able to retrieve it. (And, of course, he lost the great love of his life, never to retrieve her—Ava Gardner.)

The antipodal position of love is "lonely." No one Thrives being alone. One can only Thrive in others' company.

---

[62] Whenever someone asks, after I walk off the stage, if they can provide feedback about my speech, I say, "No," and keep on walking. They want to play "gotcha" and I'm not interested.

These five traits—resilience, eternal learning, self-esteem, perseverance, and love—constitute the armory for Thriving. One can easily nominate others, such as faith, courage, forgiveness, or creativity. But I've found that these are the core required to Thrive.

However, no matter whether you add to my list or substitute, the real question is: What are you doing to acquire, perpetuate, and develop those traits? Are you taking the time and making the effort to gain and apply the traits that I've recommended or that you feel are essential to your well being, growth, and happiness?

Do you have the time and inclination to create this reality for yourself, or are you too easily sidetracked and derailed?[63] Or are you uncertain as to what constitutes your true engagement, and whether "bigger" is always better?

Out next chapter will help you to sort that out.

---

[63] The comedian Steven Wright said that he'd love to be able to daydream, but he always gets distracted.

CHAPTER 10

TIAABB:
There is always a bigger boat

Are others controlling your happiness?

During a trip to St. Barth's, we found six $25 million yachts parked bumper-to-bumper in the harbor. There were another dozen in the bay which couldn't find room—or perhaps couldn't fit—in the harbor. It was like viewing a boring boat show, with little variation and simply size as a distinguishing feature, which itself was rather common.

There is *always* a bigger boat. If you think you've found the largest, someone will build a bigger one. Someone will have a nicer car, a better vacation spot, a more successful kid, a grander résumé.

Who cares? I don't, and neither should you. If you want to Thrive, focus on your personal happiness, not your relative position to others.

Wealth is more about discretionary time than money

Life is not about the "best," "most," or "biggest." It's about what makes you happy. There are three key words there: "what," "you," and "happy."

What I've learned is that true wealth is about discretionary time. Your ability to go where you want, to engage in what you want, when you want, is quite powerful. You can always make another dollar, but you can't make another minute. Time is not a resource issue (we get a new 24 hours daily) but rather a *priority* issue. The question is how we choose to spend the time, or whether we can even engage in that decision.

Fresh out of undergraduate school, I went to work for Prudential Insurance in Newark, NJ. I was a refugee from a law school scholarship that forced me to realize I desperately did not want to become a lawyer. So at the last minute, the placement counselor got me into a hot shot management program at the Pru.

What I most remember, even in the days of strict punctuality and bells which indicated breaks and lunch, that I was still shocked that I was a prisoner. When I looked down at the street six floors below, I realized that I was prohibited from walking out there before or after lunch unless I took a vacation day or a sick day! I had near-zero discretionary time. Somewhere in the recesses of my brain was formed the nascent idea that this was very, very bad.

When I was recruited by a consulting firm in Princeton, I was subjected to heavy travel for the first time in my young life. Ironically, however, my discretionary time increased, because no one was watching the clock at the office, and the travel had the pleasant offset of being home for my kids' dance recital or soccer game on a Wednesday afternoon. (I was the only father generally present, and the rumors began that I was somehow involved in drugs, which was vaguely true, since Merck was a big client!)

When I hear people today say things like, "I wish I could go to my kid's soccer game, but I have no time," or "I'd love to go shopping with you and give you my advice, but I can't fit it in," I conclude that the person chooses not to go to the game or to shop. In this vastly more informal world, we have a great deal more discretion. But are we spending it glued to the often ridiculous social media platforms, merely simulating relationships? Or are we squandering it at the behest of someone else's tacit or implicit request for you to make that sacrifice?

Ironically, I've observed that many entrepreneurs who leave large organizations to strike out on their own and form their own business, actually go to work for a much tougher, harsher, less flexible boss!

Moreover, *if you work hard merely to make money, you can actually be working hard to decrease your wealth.* Money is fuel for life, and the real wealth in life is discretionary time. Call it "self-directed time." The more you must mindlessly work, travel, and respond to others, the less your wealth, no matter how much money you're earning.

Do you really envy lawyers who need to work 90 hours a week (even 60, once you take out the padding and the lies) in order to churn out enough billable hours to justify their overhead and create a profit? That's the craziest philosophy I've ever seen, and how someone can spend three years in law school, pass a tough bar exam, and bill like an idiot is simply beyond me.

Grinding away to have the "biggest" or the "best" or the "most" is more than just crazy. The key is: What makes you happy? Not someone else's "stuff," and not in comparison to someone else and their stuff.

If you're incapable of comprehending what makes you happy without comparing yourself to others, you're suffering from the vacuum effect that is sweeping you through life too fast for you to consider your condition. You've become inured to what's "best" for you from the media, from others, from fiction, and from a very narrow perspective. One of the reasons I favor travel so much is that you're able to meet a lot of happy people around the globe who have far less than you do, and often don't care.

"Things" (or as comedian George Carlin said, "stuff") are not inherently wrong or bad. But they cannot constitute your criteria for success. They are means to ends, not ends. Collecting art because the aesthetics are pleasing and the pursuit is educational is one thing, but collecting it because you want the same as or more than others in your economic strata is an exercise in burning money and time.

Alan's Discretionary Time Questions

- How much discretionary time do I truly have in an average week?

- How many people are able to successfully divert your time through orders, requests, or guilt?

- How often do you find yourself regretting that you've missed a family event?

- How often do you find yourself regretting that you've missed an entertainment or recreational opportunity?

- How many items are on your formal or informal list of things you'd like to do that you haven't been able to get to for over a year?

- To what extent are you "addicted" to meetings, online activities, and social responsibilities that aren't highly pleasurable but constitute "obligations" of formal or informal nature?

- To what extent do you strive to obtain things which others have, which you hadn't thought about doing prior to that exposure?

- How many things do you own that you made a special effort to acquire which you don't use often or at all?

- To what extent do you refer to certain activities and earlier investments as "a good idea at the time" but not so much any more?

- How often are you involved in one-upmanship about a purchase, a trip, an experience, or an achievement?

- How much of your time do you spend longing for things because others have them?

- How much of the time do you spend simply madly happy about what you currently have?

I'm not going to bother to tell you how to score this: I think you get the idea! Are you able to say that you're leading a contented life, or are others and their criteria determining the extent to which you're happy and content?

Happiness is synthetic, not organic

If you visit TED, one of the truly outstanding Internet resources,[64] you can watch Harvard psychologist Dan Gilbert explain his theories of happiness. One of the most profound, I believe, is that it is more synthetic than organic. In other words, you can create your own happiness.

I once thought such an idea was pure rationalization. People who claim that "the car accident was the best thing that ever happened to me," and "as I look back, I'm so glad I lost that job," were, I believed, engaged in deep self-deception. "Natural" happiness, after all, is about the empirical, non-judgmental elations: successfully married, well employed, respected and liked, sufficient leisure time, and so on.

Then you realize that you've become a Stepford Wife.

Gilbert points out that self-created happiness is not an exercise in rationalization, or at least not a harmful one. It's a way to keep oneself "up" and positive and motivated. If you regret the job loss or the house move or the school not attended without surcease or limit, then by the time you're into adulthood you're dragging around enough baggage to require the purchase of a forklift.

However, if you position a drawback, setback, or not being the starting quarterback as something that was ultimately positive—since the episode allowed for another path to emerge, another opportunity to unfold, another important relationship to develop—then life's vicissitudes can be organized into positive results. The world isn't out to

[64] www.ted.com /speakers/dan_gilbert.html

get you. You can make lemonade, and there is a pony somewhere in the room.

We have all encountered people who are determined to spoil their day and ours. I've walked into coffee shops at the beach at 7 am to find the counter help surly and brusque. Imagine beginning your day that way—it's not going to improve—in a job that is the exact same every day without variance? Most government workers are withdrawn and morose. (Why wouldn't they be in those jobs?) But it's not a contagion. Anyone who flies frequently knows that most TSA security people range from prison guards to ushers. Some are power-driven, some are cordial. *They each make their own personal environment.*

They can each make their own happiness.

A lousy customer (and I'll grant that those who work behind the counter meet some awful customers) can turn into a funny story. Broken dishes come with the turf. A passenger with a large scissor in a piece of hand luggage is more oblivious than dangerous. When a seagull has christened my car overnight at the beach, I ask myself if I can write about it in a column while I get the polish I keep just for that purpose out of the trunk. I don't curse the fates and scream, "Why ME??!!"

Happiness and life balance are about what makes sense for you.[65] There is no objective set of "happiness criteria" by which you gauge your current state of elation. The neighbor's possessions, your Long Island cousin's free time, your work colleague's advanced degree, and the latest "hot" vacation destination touted in a magazine have no bearing on your state of happiness, unless you voluntarily surrender your life to others' possessions, destinations, and intentions.

---

[65] Without going to extremes. At my Life Balance Workshop, an attorney asked me what was wrong with 80 hours a week serving clients if he loved the work, had no other interests, and was good at it. I asked if he had a family. "Yes, a wife and two boys," he replied. "That's what's wrong with it," I pointed out.

TIAABB: You're not going to be happy if you mindlessly pursue what you perceive makes others happy (especially since many of them are mindlessly pursuing what's making still someone else supposedly happy—this stuff is viral). It's fine to make yourself happy even when conventional wisdom may dictate you've had a mild disaster!

I call this "personalized happiness." After all, the alternative is often glumness and festering self-pity.

I was fired in 1985 by a boss who was clueless. I didn't get much severance, didn't have much money in the bank, was looking at a lousy economy, and had major bills. It seemed to me that the best course of action was to admit that this was the best thing that could have happened to me, and charge onward. Things haven't been too bad since.

I'm not suggesting that a broken toe is a signal for celebration, or that a lost opportunity is a sign of success. But I am contending that life is not so much about what happens to you, but rather what you do about what happens to you. (Most "motivational speakers" stop right there. I'm here to tell you *what* to do about it!)

When my son didn't get the lead in the final play of his undergraduate theater career, he was momentarily devastated. I told him that he could protest to the dean, organize his classmates to withdraw, scream at the head of the department, or take a subordinate role and absolutely shine, while receiving credit for his maturity in light of the disappointment. He did the last and has never looked back.

We create our own happiness, and that of others. We have no more right to consume happiness without creating it than we do to consume wealth without creating it. To what extent are you looking at the filled glass and not the empty one, the opportunity and not the threat, the lesson learned instead of the deep disappointment?

Personalized happiness is completely within your control and available 24 hours a day. There's a reason that people so often say, "It was for the best," even in the death of a loved one. They just want to be happy.

Success always trumps perfection

I'm a great believer in therapy, especially when it's not in reaction to a trauma or problem. During one such session, in response to my griping about something not going exactly the way I had intended, the therapist (as I mentioned at $110 per hour!) says to me, "For goodness' sake, Alan, it's about success, not perfection."

That was a breakthrough moment.

I tell people that they should be able to write an article or position paper in two hours. They tell me they need two weeks, and I shouldn't assume they have my "gifts." (If I had "gifts" I'd be another John Updike.)

I tell people that they should be able to speak out in a social setting to establish their point of view. They tell me they might say the wrong thing.

I tell people they should be happy with what they've accomplished. They tell me that they had planned to do much more, or someone else has already done much more.

That's why I had such a breakthrough moment. These people are burning up time and energy on the impossible pursuit of perfection.

I herein introduce you to a different kind of 80/20 rule.

In the graphic on the next page, I'm advocating that you don't even bother trying to come close to perfection. At 80 percent readiness, you move. That's because the final 20 percent requires a huge expenditure of additional time *without proportional return for the investment.*

- The final 20 percent I could put into this book the reader wouldn't even notice as missing now.

- The final 20 percent you plan for a speech will be lost on the audience.

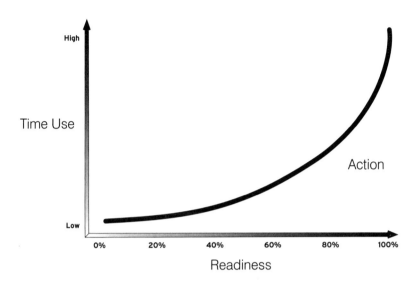

80 percent ready, move

- The final 20 percent you put into cleaning the garage will make neither an aesthetic nor functional difference.

- The final 20 percent you invest is the social interaction will probably be perceived as over-the-top.

There is always a bigger boat, so enlarging or improving the one you have by the final 20 percent will neither make it more pleasing to you not make it the biggest boat. The search for an arbitrary perfection, where you can't "win enough" or be "prepared enough" or "impress enough" is the pursuit of the impossible and unachievable—the unfulfilled in pursuit of the unattainable. Baseball pitchers don't take the mound trying for a perfect game. They try to do the best they can that day under those conditions. On rare occasions—when no one makes an error, when the other team isn't hitting well, when someone makes an extraordinary catch, when the opposing manager makes some dumb moves—perfection may be achieved. But in the entire history of the

World Series, there has been only one such game, and less than two dozen in all the statistic-crazed history of professional baseball.

A horse that wins a race by a nose wins 10 times the purse of the second place horse with the smaller honker. Yet that winner didn't practice 10 times as much, or have 10 times the blood lines, or have a jockey 10 times better (or lighter). You only have to win by a nose to make 10 times the purse. You don't have to set records and you don't have to be the best ever.[66] You simply have to win. A four-game sweep is the same as a seven-game win in the bottom of the final inning for the baseball championship. Winning prizefighters are often as battered as the defeated opponent. The reward isn't in being unscathed, it's in being left standing at the conclusion.

I once heard a "big name" speaker, whom most of you would recognize in a minute, tell a convention of aspiring speakers that he practiced two hours for every one hour of his actual presentation, every time. Everyone knew he only had one speech, and he had been delivering it for 20 years, probably twice a week. So he had been spending thousands upon thousands of hours practicing a speech that most people in the audience could recite from memory (and, in fact, he repeated one ubiquitous, inane story that had become a parody, but which he has never realized as such). He told the audience that he called his preparation "a professional habit."

I call it a learning disability.

The search for perfection is the same search as trying to have the biggest boat—it ain't gonna happen.

The intent to reach perfection is a more socially acceptable alternative to its real intent: procrastination. An imperfect article on your website is better than no article; taking your kid to a ball game of minor league teams is better than no ballgame together at all; fixing the washing

---

[66] The difference between the winning golfer and the golfer who comes in tenth in professional tournaments is less than a stroke a round, for example.

machine is better than doing without until you can afford a new state-of-the-art washer.

Of course, I realize that *you* wouldn't be a procrastinator, and that *you* aren't concerned with a debilitating search for perfection. But in case you want to check out a "friend," have your "friend" take this test.

Alan's Test for Irrational Perfection

1. Do you tend to rewrite endlessly, including three-line "thank you" notes?

2. Are you afraid to speak out because others are better at it than you?

3. Do you take many photos of the exact same shot to try to capture the perfect angle, moment, or lighting?

4. Do you refuse to let people record your voice because you don't like the way you sound?

5. Do you refuse to be photographed unless you're positive you look "exactly right"?

6. Do you change clothes several times before deciding on an outfit?

7. Do you wait—often for years, when it's gone out of style—before wearing something just purchased because you seek "the perfect event or time"?

8. Do you go crazy when you discover the car, a piece of furniture, or your lawn has a minor imperfection or two?

9. Are you upset if your kids receive less than perfect grades?

10. Do you change your tickets and/or seats when you realize that you could have better ones, even only marginally better ones?

11. Are you irritated when there is less than total silence among the theater audience, at the business meeting, or on public transportation?

12. If something minor but unexpected occurs, such as a spill, or a lost memory button on your car radio, do you feel you must stop everything and fix it immediately?

13. Do you keep buying new stereos, phones, or cable boxes every time you suspect that someone else has a better sound system or reception?

14. If someone doesn't use a directional system, do you at least consider taking down their license plate and turning them into the police?[67]

15. Are you seldom content with your attire, hair color, hair style, lack of hair, makeup, accessories, and/or posture?

Scoring

- If you answered "yes" one time or more, you (that is, your friend) have dangerously dysfunctional perfectionist tendencies. You are fruitlessly searching for a bigger boat.

If you want to Thrive, you have to be happy—synthetically happy, if you will—with success. That horse doesn't say, "Only won by a nose, I need to do better next time or I'll be in the glue factory." He says, "Wow, still another win, glad I didn't have to expend myself more, because that stud farm is looking better and better right now!"

At least, I think that's what he's saying. I know I would be.

---

[67] Readers from Rhode Island may skip this question, since no one in Rhode Island *ever* uses turn signals.

Happiness is *not* just a thing called "dough"

Harold Arlen wrote a little ditty, sung by Judy Garland and a raft of other chanteuses, called, "Happiness Is Just A Thing Called Joe." The premise is that Joe made the woman content, nothing else needed.

I don't make that claim about money—"dough"—which I feel is actually just fuel for life. But if you consider synthetic happiness, and that there is always a bigger boat, then we should be able to put money in perspective. Striving to amass as much as possible isn't very bright or rewarding, in and of itself. But acquiring enough to support a constructive and rewarding lifestyle makes a lot of sense.

I used to love the old Scrooge McDuck comic books. (My mother disposed of my treasure trove once I got married, more fuel for the therapist's fires.) He kept his money in a vault as large as an apartment building (not a bad idea in some investment economies we've seen) and periodically dove in and burrowed around in it, like a demented mole. The Beagle Boys kept trying to rob him since, obviously, they knew where the money was, but he stubbornly insisted on keeping it in one place.

He was also a miser, one of his more disagreeable attributes, aside from not taking care of Donald, Huey, Dewey, and Louie.

There are a few human qualities which I consider to be vile and insidious, and one of them is cheapness. I think one has the right to earn and accumulate money, but I also think that the money should be spent and invested in lifestyle, charity, legacy, and community. I don't mind people who amass and spend money, but I am revolted by people who amass money just for the sake of it.

Scrooge McDuck made for an amusing comic book figure, but not a very good uncle or friend.

What *does* your Thriving lifestyle consist of, and what investment does it require? There are seven categories to consider when evaluating your needs for a Thriving lifestyle:

1. What are my basic preferred living costs (mortgage, utilities, transportation, insurance, food, clothing, and so forth)?

2. What are my personal lifestyle additions (vacations, jewelry, cars, appearance, recreation, and so on)?

3. What are my planning needs costs (marriage, children, education, retirement, and so on)?

4. What are my contribution costs (charities, arts, political, community, and so on)?

5. What kind of reserve or contingency for the unexpected do I need (normally a minimum of six months of basic living costs)?

6. What kind of "wish list" needs would I like to support (new job, move, boat, better car, additional travel, and so on)?

7. What kind of legacy do I want to leave, and to whom, beyond whatever is in my estate (special bequests, prized possessions, grandchildren's trust, and so forth)?

That list is both pretty interesting and pretty frightening once you attach actual dollars to the plans and aspirations. But it's nothing more than you normally consider consciously or subconsciously, on a piecemeal basis. I'm simply suggesting that you take a holistic and comprehensive view of your financial needs.

Money doesn't equate to happiness, but neither is it "the root of all evil." It's neither anodyne nor panacea. If you give an unhappy person more money, they tend to be a wealthier, unhappy person.

But money does provide for economic power. And, like it or not, this is a capitalistic society and capitalistic world. That means, in short, you need capital. I'm suggesting that you admit it and get organized about it.

People require varying amounts, just as the responses to my seven questions above will generate varying results. And money—the fuel for life—comes in differing forms: present cash, future cash, assets, and credit. Despite every economic crisis in the world, don't debunk legitimate credit. It is meant to fill in spots where there is uneven or insufficient cash flow *when you are confident that future cash will repay the credit.* (People who refuse to go into debt aren't frugal or smart, they don't trust themselves to repay, don't foresee the future cash, or are simply anal.) Since the dawn of currency, people have intelligently used credit to offset temporary shortfalls in cash. I couldn't have begun or sustained my business without the intelligent use of credit.

Neither could FedEx, IBM, or Wal-Mart. And, oops, neither can the federal government or most local governments. Credit isn't evil. Its use in lieu of *available and future cash* is irresponsible. If you borrow and can't expect to repay, then it's not the credit that's the problem, it's you.

Back to economic power: Money is a means to more rapidly and effectively achieve ends. Having the money to pay for your kids' college (or private school—category #2 above) educations is better than having to depend on unpredictable scholarships. You can choose better schools, make decisions earlier, and gain favored consideration. Paying your bills promptly with local small businesses will gain you easier access when you need a rush job done or non-standard treatment. Enduring a non-insured loss (#5 above) is much more palatable and less stressful when you have the cash to pay for it without sacrificing or going into debt when you don't see the future cash to cover the borrowed amount.

Clinical psychologist Frederick Herzberg theorized that the presence of money is not a motivator, but the absence of money is a demotivator.[68] He called this "hygiene theory." If you extrapolate this,

---

[68] See, for example, Frederick Herzberg's book, *Work and the Nature of Man* (World Publishing, 1966).

the presence of money does not ensure happy relationships, or success in endeavors, or rewarding friendships. But the absence of money and the concomitant stress almost always weakens and threatens relationships, work, and plans. The lack of money creates a sense of powerlessness, and powerlessness is corrupting and devastating.

I've waited until this point in the book—I hope having created a dynamic and understanding that puts the following in perspective—to present the unavoidable fact that money will help you to Thrive. Not all the money in the world, not necessarily a bigger boat than the neighbors, but enough money to fulfill the seven categories of need above adjusted for your lifestyle and aspirations.

People tend to wish their lives away: "If only I could have...." "I wish I had been able to...." "Under better circumstances I would have...." A great deal of that phenomenon, which is debilitating and based on victimology, is caused by a lack or means, a lack of resources, a lack of finances.

A lack of cash.

Money won't make you happy, unless you're like Scrooge McDuck and simply love to wallow in it. But it will provide the power you need in life to realize your aspirations. You can't very well take care of others if you don't take care of yourself. That is not a selfish rationalization. It is a safety rule on airplanes.[69] The government endorses it. History supports it.

And I'm here to tell you that, while true wealth is discretionary time, the fuel for that wealth and for your life is the ability to earn and acquire money commensurate with your reasonable financial needs and lifestyle.

Fortunately, we live in a society where that is eminently possible, and the ability to Thrive is omnipresent.

---

[69] "Put your own oxygen mask on first," our topic earlier.

The Runner

Now let me tell you why you needn't even win by a nose to be successful, an example of hope to others, and create excitement.

In the 1950s, in Union City, New Jersey, there was an athletic stadium
built during the Depression by the Works Progress Administration
called, of course, Roosevelt Field. (It was on Roosevelt Boulevard.)
Union City was then, and is now, one of the most densely populated
cites in the country, with about 50,000 citizens crammed into about
two square miles. It was at the time a working class, blue collar neigh-
borhood of European immigrants and second generation Americans,
in that respect, not unlike ten thousand others.

Roosevelt Stadium was torn down in 2008 to make way for a new high
school (that was too small for the enrollment on the day it opened,
such was the planning in Union City). However, during the time of
my story, it occupied a precious six square blocks, equaled only by the
Catholic Monastery then in operation.[70]

On July 4, Independence Day, each year, Roosevelt Stadium hosted
day-long events, culminating in fireworks at night. Admission was free,
and with a quarter you could get two hot dogs and a soda, so the seats
filled up quickly in the half-moon seating of the accommodations for
about 4,000 people. There we would plant ourselves, after a 12-block
walk, and watch baton twirlers, sack races, singing groups, horses, and
all the random bits of Americana that are displayed when people aren't
in school or at work and are seeking inexpensive entertainment.

The highlight of the day, however, was the later afternoon half-mile
invitational race. On the cinder track of Roosevelt Stadium's field (because a cinder track was cheap) were standing on this day six of the
finest half-milers in Hudson County's school system, and there were
some great high school athletes in Hudson County.

---

[70] The gorgeous gothic edifice is still there on West Street but is now the home
of condominiums, still another example of less than infinite wisdom by the
city fathers.

Two of the runners were known to be far and away the cream of the crop, and we settled in for a tough race between them as the starter's gun went off in the seating end of the stadium. Since there were no staggered starts, the runners immediately bunched to try to get to the inside.

On the first turn, in a tangle of arms and legs, one of the two favorites crashed face first into the cinders and lay there for a couple of seconds. The crowd groaned, seeing the tight race disappear on the first turn, but cheered on this Runner as he jumped up and pursued the pack now coming into the first straightaway.

The Runner ran at a sprint, not a half-mile pace, and was soon a decent sixth. But we all knew that he couldn't keep up a sprinter's pace for the entire race. Going into the second turn, he passed the fifth place runner on the outside. You're never supposed to pass on the outside of a turn to conserve energy, but we realized he felt he had no choice. In the second straightaway, completing the first of two laps on the quarter mile track, he moved into fourth. And on the third turn, where he originally fell, he passed again on the outside, at a furious pace, to move into a now-distant third.

The crowd began to come to life. While we knew he couldn't keep up this torrid pace, he had already proved a great deal to us. We hoped he could at least finish third.

Then, on the fourth and final turn, he passed the second runner on the outside and, heading into the home stretch with 100 yards to go, he was moving toward his competitor in the lead, and right into the well of the stadium and 4,000 incredulous people.

As a single person, the audience rose and roared. The lead runner then did something you are never to do in racing, he looked over his shoulder. And, though clearly surprised by his pursuer, he did something you are supposed to do: He went into his finishing kick, since he still had a lot in reserve.

Incredibly, amazingly, the Runner also found a finishing kick from somewhere deep in his very soul, and with 25 yards left, he was 10 yards back; with 10 yards left, he was 2 yards back. Then, at the finish line, the Runner threw himself at the tape, landing once again face-first in the cinders of Roosevelt Stadium.

He didn't "win," he was about a foot short, but that didn't matter to the crowd. They rushed the railings and ran onto the track. Men hoisted children on their shoulders. People screamed for the Runner.

He didn't win the race, he finished second. But he showed us something, in front of our eyes, that few of us had ever so dramatically witnessed. He was a black man who couldn't in those days walk safely on our streets in the evening, or eat in some restaurants. But he showed all of us what heroism, and courage, and pride are all about.

I can't recall his name, but I'll never forget what he did that day. He's been an inspiration to me for the rest of my life. Trying to emulate his grit and determination have made me very happy, very successful, and very thankful on countless occasions during my life.

Fortunately, not even Union City can tear down lessons and memories.

CHAPTER 11

Making your dreams come true

Make it so

You can easily dream your life away. But the other side of the equation is that you can make your dreams come true. Dreaming your life away, the negative, is about what and how you think you should have said, should have done, should have responded. But fulfilling your dreams, the positive, is about your grasp meeting your reach.

I'll conclude this book on Thriving by delineating exactly how you can dream, not your life away, but your life into being. My favorite order in *Star Trek: Next Generation* was phlegmatically uttered by Captain Picard, "Make it so."

Here's how you can "make it so"—even if you don't have the crew of the Enterprise on the bridge.

Move three things forward a mile, not a hundred things forward an inch

One of the hallmarks of bright, intellectually curious people is that they love to jump from one cool interest to the next before not quite finishing with the first. Like a water bug skimming the surface so that it doesn't sink, smart people like to keep moving so that they don't get too deep into anything and become stuck (or drown).

I can't blame them, but I can help them.

I don't believe that you tackle things sequentially. That is, you can't wait to fix the roof until the garage is spotlessly clean, and you can't wait to study for the psychology test until the statistics exam is successfully negotiated. You can't wait to travel to Tibet or study the oboe until your kids are grown and gainfully employed (or Lhasa would be even more isolated and symphony orchestras would be missing a key woodwind).

However, there is a limit to how much you can undertake concurrently. I'm talking major projects and initiatives here, not the humdrum banality of everyday living. (Psychologists will tell you not to undertake too much change at once, e.g., losing your job, moving your home, having elective surgery, putting your spouse on an ice floe for the polar bears.) Thus, moving three things forward a mile trumps moving a hundred things forward by an inch.

Now, if you accompany this with my "80 percent ready, move" philosophy from an earlier chapter, you can see that this isn't as daunting (or frustrating) as you might fear. You needn't "complete" your preparedness, but you do need to launch.

For instance, if you're trying to market a new service, then get your website in good shape, target your natural buyers, and tell everyone you know what you're doing. But don't also try, simultaneously, to open a new office, hire administrative help, and launch a series of workshops. Similarly, if you're attempting to learn to sail, then rent a boat, hire an instructor, and take a marine safety course. But put on a back burner refurbishing the boat, finding better dock space, and looking to buy your own boat. (TIAABB). In my vernacular, three things at a time that can be done concurrently. Not everything can, of course.

There is a famous story of Union Army General George B. McClellan, a martinet and egoist, later to run against Lincoln in his second term (we all know what happened there), who was found by a newspaper reporter to be dictating three letters simultaneously to three different secretaries. It was a wondrous phenomenon. But later all three letters had to be re-dictated.

If you want to realize even your wildest dreams, you have to be under control. Garages, desks, offices, diaries, and cerebellums are full of abandoned projects, partially pursued plans, and unfulfilled dreams. No one gets much credit for the half-built boat in the garage, the inadequate funds raised to support a bid for public office, or the catalogs gathering dust for the excursion to Marrakesh.

One reason for unfulfilled dreams we've covered earlier: The search for perfection instead of success. It's better to have a vacation in Florida than not take one in the Caribbean because you only have enough money to go to Florida and have to wait to get the extra cash to....

The other reason, however, is having too many things afire on the front burners.

Congress has a tough time passing bills, as does every state legislature. The inevitable result is the frenzy of midnight sessions as the term ends trying to cram down as much of the overflowing paperwork as possible, without much debate or quality. Analysis: No one would complain if National Belt Day were put off for a few decades if decent health care provisions could be passed in the meantime.

If you want to Thrive, you must organize to get things done.

Here are my tips to do that.

Alan's Charge Ahead Principles

- **If you want to see things through to completion, start at the end**. Choose a results point, an ending date, an outcome time—whatever you choose to call it, and work backwards. Hence, if you want to clean out the garage, assign a date: October 1. Then work backwards to today: July 1. Decide what you have to do in July, August, and September (e.g., throw out the old stuff, repaint, new shelving, new door, new floor, heating, etc.). Allocate your time and investments accordingly. (Obviously, you can't do too many such projects at once or your calendar will be crammed.)

- **Provide rewards at mileposts**. As you achieve key steps (a chapter completed, a new floor installed, reservations confirmed) give yourself a present. Walk the dog, hit the beach, buy a memento, make furious love. (These are *not* concurrent.)

- **Pursue and secure resources**. If you need workers, or colleagues, or painters, or time, or access to information, arrange for it to be ready when you are. One of the greatest causes on not being able to charge ahead is that you're always waiting on something to happen or someone to appear. It's better to have the equipment taking up space in storage than it is for you to be all dressed up with nothing to use.

- **Eschew distractions**. Feel free to put alluring and enticing new ideas and requests on a list, on a back burner, or under a refrigerator magnet, but do not allow the siren to undermine you. You can get to the new thing. Aside from illness and tragedy, all else can usually wait. Consider: If everything is a priority, nothing is a priority. The three things you want to move forward a mile are your actual priorities. Accord them that respect and investment.

- **Assign another major initiative or project as you complete a prior one**. So long as you aren't pursuing perfection but success, your major issues will be dealt with, will be reconciled, will end. Then you can add another. This keeps the circulation going and your own need for variety fulfilled.

We tend to allow a surfeit of small things to overwhelm our small amount of really big things. Thriving is based on finding ways to realize our most important personal and professional objectives.

Signs of a hundred things inching forward:

- A cluttered desk that looks like something blew up.
- A calendar filled with back-to-back, wall-to-wall activities.
- A feeling of total lack of progress on any given day.
- A raft of messages asking you where something is or how you're doing.
- A loss of key information and/or continuity as you switch from one thing to another.
- A repetition of the same items on your priority lists, which tends to be quite long.

Stop trying to do everything, especially at once. Make it so.

The power of Tools for Change: The 1% Solution®

The way to Thrive is one day, one issue, one interaction at a time. Affirmations are dumb because they simply imply that thinking about the goals will get you there. If that were true, you could get from New York to LA without United Airlines and with dramatically less assault on your baggage, liquids, and shoes.

The reality is that we need steps and mileposts to reach our goals and, counterintuitively, they can be small. "Think big" is fine for identifying the destination, but "think of the next move" is important for progress toward it. How many people have you talked about over the years, personally and professionally, who are said to be a "terrific big picture thinker, but not much of an innovator." Here are the euphemisms:

- Doesn't follow through.
- Overlooks details.
- Leaves the implementation to others.
- Fails to implement.
- Moves on too quickly.

Strategy, visions, results, outcomes—these can be big picture, and singular. But the means to get there—tactics, plans, implementation, execution, administration—they need to be routinized.

That's because if you improve by just 1 percent a day, in 70 days you're twice as good.[71] Not enough people I've known do this with regularity and persistence. Too few clients have accomplished it. Government projects tend not to come close to it. Imagine if our ability to tend to veterans' affairs, or the administration of social security, or simplification of the tax code, improved by just 1 percent a day? Or even a month? Or even.....well, you get the idea.

If you want to play an instrument, you need to improve a small bit at a time, but methodically. A good teacher can put the right sequence and priorities together for you: reading music, understanding the keyboard, finding notes, using the pedals, changing chords, whatever. The same applies to learning how to speak well publicly: creating notes, using the stage, including examples, handling questions, and so forth. When I first tried to learn to play tennis, a guy kept showing me how to serve, which I found nearly impossible to master. I looked like a demented fly swatter. Only later did I learn that professionals spent hours just on the ball toss!

It's tough to Thrive when you're in a rut. And let me define rut: It's doing more and more of what you're already pretty good at, without advancing your technique, effectiveness, or success. Tiger Woods, Meryl Streep, Frank Sinatra, Michael Jordon, Picasso, Lincoln, Edison, Jonas Salk—they are or were all pursuing their sustaining 1 percent.

I call this "Tools for Change" because that periodic, small but inexorable improvement will ironically propel you toward your goal. That United flight has to fly past Chicago (and unfortunately, sometimes

---

[71] This is a derivation of the law of compound interest, but if you don't believe me, enter "1" in your calculator, the multiply it by 1.01 70 times and you'll arrive at......2!

has to land at O'Hare) on the way to LA. Can't avoid it. You can't play the piano without knowing the tune and where to find the keys. You're not going to close the speech to thunderous applause without a few things happening after "Good morning."

I've found that people tend to get frustrated because they can't fit the entire enchilada in their mouths. You have to take one bite at a time.

Here are areas in which to examine your systematic 1 percent opportunities for improvement and advancement toward larger goals:

- Professionally, are you learning more about your work, your job, your career?

- Are you advancing and gaining more pleasure from your hobbies and pastimes?

- Do you handle relationships better?

- Are you able to resolve conflict quickly and successfully?

- Are you reducing your stress level?

- Are you improving your fitness and health?

- Are you removing self-created impediments to your goals?

- Are you removing external impediments to your goals?

- Are you saving and creating resources necessary to your plans and accountabilities?

- Are you preparing for loss and life changes?

- Is your discretionary time increasing?

Let's tackle one of these as an example: conflict resolution. That is part of a larger goal, which may be termed "building effective relationships" or "building influence" or whatever you choose to call it. In this particular subset, let's identify that conflict resolutions is, 90 percent of the time, over objectives (destinations) or alternatives (routes).[72] In other words, we may disagree on the destination (the mountains for the beach for vacation) or the route (we agree on the beach, but do we drive, fly, take the scenic route, the expressway, and so on).

Conflict over alternatives is best resolved by focusing on the common, shared, agreed upon objective to defuse hostility, and then comparing the pros and cons of the alternatives, choosing one, combining several, or coming up with a new one. Conflict over objectives is best resolved by determining who best "owns" the decision (e.g., "Where would the kids be happiest?") and relying on that common goal.

Just knowing and organizing around these principles, then practicing them, may take a few days or weeks, but the steady progress will produce the 1 percent multiplier, until you're quite adept. (And that, in turn, produces a 1 percent in the larger issue of "building influence," for example.)

The same applies to self-created impediments to your goal. Are you removing/improving at 1 percent a day? You don't do that by saying, "I need to improve my self-esteem." You do it by taking a class in self-esteem, or getting a coach, or going to therapy, and then following the guidance.

The good news and the bad news is that it takes only 1 percent a day, because while that sounds eminently achievable, it also denies you the excuse of volume, magnitude, and overwhelm. The sad reason that most people cannot make their dreams come true has more to do with procrastination than inability; delay rather than obstacle; lassitude instead of immovable objects.

Captain Piccard figured out his options as a leader, then told First Officer Riker (or anyone else under his command who could influence the outcome) to "make it so." We are our own Picards. Our own Rikers.

---

[72] The rest of the time it may be truly interpersonal and behavioral, but this is actually relatively rare, despite the oft-claimed "chemistry differences."

We can "make it so" ourselves. Do you remember Scotty, down in the engine room, in the original episodes? He kept warning that the reactors would explode, or the warp drive would implode, but somehow he managed to get it done, to follow the captain's orders, to "make it so."

We only have to make it so one day at a time, 1 percent at a time, which doesn't sound very intimidating at all, does it?

So the question is, "What's stopping you?" You need to improve in any given area at 1 percent a day to double your effectiveness in 70 days. You're not going to find a faster, surer route anywhere.

It's the royal road to Thriving.

Avoid the feedback pinball machine

I have delivered the keynote addresses at the National Speakers Association national conventions in Melbourne, Ottawa, New Orleans, and Birmingham over four consecutive years. I don't know if anyone else has ever done that. It's rewarding, but you get a lot of......feedback.

Unsolicited feedback is for the sender, not the receiver. It is a way of saying, "You may have accomplished that or achieved this or been lauded by them, but I have some ways you can improve, because I know more than you do." Those who say that the only thing to do with feedback is to listen to it have obviously never tried to use it, because they would otherwise be trying to lift their left leg and right leg at the same time without falling.

After my Birmingham opening general session, I was ushered into a small reception. Sure enough, a man approached me—a "speech coach," who else?—and asked if he could give me feedback.

"Is there anything in what remains of the entire British Empire that could stop you?" I calmly asked. He continued, oblivious to the sarcasm, because those who give unsolicited feedback never listen to it themselves.

"When you walked about the stage," he didactically continued, "I didn't focus on any of your points. But, when you stood in one spot, I absorbed everything you were saying. Do you know what that's called?"

"A learning deficiency?" I ventured.

You must inure yourself to those "trying to help you." First, most of them are really not and are at best apathetic to whether you're being helped. (The passive/aggressives actually want you to be hurt.) Second, most of them are not qualified to offer the feedback, either in the content or the context. Third, most of them will send you down an almost irretrievable side-track of old trains and abandoned factories.

"Most of them" = 99 percent

If you want to make your dreams come true you cannot allow yourself to subscribe to others' dreams at their request. Virtually all unsolicited feedback is from people with an agenda: They are anal about typos, they think that a speech must be delivered without notes, they believe you can't start a sentence with "but," they don't feel you can wear white after Labor Day. BUT these are not your big picture thinkers.

It's tough to demur without seeming like an ingrate. After all, if they've taken the time to watch/read/hear you, then shouldn't you repay the courtesy by listening to their commentary and suggestions? Sure, but only if you have hidden ear buds playing Twisted Sister at rocket launcher decibel levels. But, I digress.

You will be a ball in that strangely hypnotic Japanese game of Pachinko if you listen to and, God forbid, follow, unsolicited feedback. Listen to one of Sinatra's songs, "They All Laughed" (George and Ira Gershwin, of course) which tells about the feedback for Columbus, Edison, Whitney, and Marconi. And they all laughed when the guy wanted to get the girl.

If you want to get the guy or the girl or the goal, ignore the com-
mentators, advisors, and laughers, *unless* you have chosen people you
respect—and who have done it before themselves—for the feedback.
That's *solicited* feedback. Never fear that, unless you have *really* lousy
judgment in friends and supporters.

If you say, "Make it so" in front of those who love to offer feedback,
they may counter with:

> "Make it so when convenient."

> "Would you mind making it so?"

> "Make it as close to 'so' as is reasonable."

> "Let's get a committee to investigate making it so."

> "Make it seemly."

> "He, she, or it should make it so."

> "Perhaps we shouldn't make it so."

> "Don't make it so much."

I've seen people's dreams ruined by those who offer "help." It's usually not malicious (though sometimes it is), it's usually done with the
intent to help, it's usually focused on "fixing" you. And it's usually
deadly.

First, we don't grow or fulfill ourselves by "fixing." We're not damaged goods. We Thrive through growth based on our strengths and
passions.

Second, there are a lot of good ways to do things. Someone else's ideal
doesn't mean that it should be yours. I've seen different, successful
golf swings; investment strategies; diets; vacation spots; speech deliver-
ies; purchasing strategies; and marital arrangements. If there is more
than a single way to perform a surgical procedure, trust me, there is
more than one way to cook a burger or wash the car.

Third, it's the height of pretension to provide advice that is not sought. In an age when people *do not* normally inform someone at a meeting that they have lettuce lodged in their incisors, why is there so much unfettered freedom to suggest a better way to present a recommendation or cook a pot roast?

Fourth, there is always another precinct to be heard from. Like some Daley, Huey Long or "Boss Haig" election night returns, there is always someone out in the boondocks with votes. If you listen to unsolicited advice that is at odds with *other* unsolicited advice, what is the critical mass to decide the day? A dozen people? A hundred? Do you take an online vote?[73]

Fifth, Who certifies the certifiers? That is, who or what accident of fate gave your eager feedback source the expertise to provide it? I always wonder who certifies those certifiers in all the "coaching universities." That "speaking coach" who cornered me in Birmingham wasn't a successful speaker or a successful coach. What law of nature says that he deserves to even get my time, much less my attention?

Sixth, you should only trust people with a vested interest in your success. Those are usually people you feel comfortable asking for feedback and advice: *People who love you, respect you, work closely with you, want you to succeed.*

Do you know how tough appropriate feedback is? Those folks who really do love you and want you to succeed usually withhold adverse feedback. When they do find themselves in a position to have to deliver it, what do we call it?

Tough love.

---

[73] This cuts both ways. One guy in Dubuque telling you that your idea for a book on management principles according to army ants is great doesn't mean you have a lock on the best-seller list, or even on your mother reading it.

There's nothing tough about unsolicited feedback from those who don't really care about you but care more about themselves, their image, their reputation, and their potential to tell others, "Yeah, I gave her some feedback that I thought she could use." That's not tough, it's easy and self-centered, and selfish.

I'm coming down hard on this because the ability to fulfill our dreams, to "make it so," and to Thrive can be (and perhaps IS being right at this moment in your life) undermined by those with purportedly good intentions but lousy help.

Avoid the feedback. Tilt the pinball machine.

Stop crying, get up, and hit someone

I curse. Sometimes loudly. I'm not proud of it. As a Catholic, I confess that I use the Lord's name in vain. I try to knock it off. But I'm not making much progress.

Then, I decided to look at it another way.

When I curse, which I try never to do when others can hear me, I am venting. I'm letting off steam—irrationally and perhaps futilely—as a safety valve would do to prevent an explosion. When I stub my toe, hit my head, lose precious copy that I was too stupid or preoccupied to back up, or forget an important event, I get angry.

Almost all anger is self-directed. We often take it out on others in order to "vent." So we get mad at a spouse or loved one, or a colleague, or a shopkeeper, or Bill Gates. (This is called "transference" in psychology.) If we don't, we tend to do damage to ourselves. Pent up anger creates huge stress, and stress creates real illness, both mental and physical.

Before EZ Pass and such automated payment systems, toll roads employed many more toll collectors. There are still some around. On a road such as the Garden State Parkway in New Jersey, these tolls are obnoxiously frequent, as if the designers said, "Let's see how often we can bring traffic to a standstill on a major roadway." Hence, some of the tolls are quite small, a quarter or 35 cents in many cases over the years (some were a dime).

When you gave some toll collectors a $20 bill for a 35 cent toll, you had an even chance of seeing a volcanic eruption in the toll booth. Why is that?

It's because you have a toll collector with no tolerance for repetition or detail, but who was placed in the position—despite the wrong behavioral predispositions for a boring, repetitive job—because he or she scored well in a test, liked the pay and benefits, wanted part-time work, knew someone who worked there, whatever. But since the actual job drove them crazy, they became quite stressed quite quickly each shift. So they essentially had two options.

They could internalize it and make themselves sick, or they could externalize it and make the customer sick.

I exaggerate to a certain degree, and I am not suggesting that this is a healthy way to handle stress, merely that it is an extreme reaction. But to return to private outbursts, not ones that threaten livestock and public transit, they can serve a purpose in alleviating pressure and unhappiness that might otherwise manifest themselves in more harmful ways.

An undergrad political science professor at Rutgers once told us that "war is simply the least subtle form of communication." It sounds somewhat bizarre, but despite never writing it down, I easily remembered the admonition.

Don't constrain yourself. There is a healthy selfishness about Thriving, and you are entitled to become angry, to be irrationally upset, *to vent in private and to mitigate your current emotional condition.* I once heard a string of obscenity from a man in the United Red Carpet Club in O'Hare when he received an obviously distressing business phone call. It was appalling. I don't condone the parents' lunatic screaming at kids' soccer games, as if the World Cup is at stake and they're hooligans in the stands.

But I do think it appropriate, in the privacy of your own existence, to yell out your displeasure. And I also think it appropriate—in fact, an emotionally healthy necessity—to intelligently vent your wrath in public.

One day my wife noticed a file on my computer within the overall correspondence file. It was titled, "complaints."

"What's in there?" she asked. I clicked on it and dozens of complaint letters were listed.

"You *wrote* all those?!"

"Yes, I'm quite proud."

When I inform a logical source of my unhappiness with their product or service (e.g., one that may be able to actually do something about my discontent) via mail, email, phone, fax, or other media, I am venting. I no longer run the risk of fretting or the injustice festering. I'm done with it. If nothing happens, I'm no worse off, but if action is taken, I'm far better off.

So I write to hotel general managers, and airline executives, and business owners, and restaurateurs, and credit card retention officers. And I have a draw full of free or discounted hotel rooms, airplane tickets, restaurant meals, and so on. I don't always get a response, and sometimes I get into a rollicking good fight.[74]

But whatever happens, I know I've done everything I can and I can get on with my life. Whether shouting in private, or calmly protesting in public, it is better than mutely suffering life's vicissitudes and is sometimes life preserving.

---

[74] The CEO of Blue Cross in Rhode Island is so annoying and pompous when questioned about company practices that I actually had discussions with the governor, assistant attorney general, and chiefs of staff of our two Senators.

At one point I argued with a doctor who was the partner of my personal physician, who was out of town. The partner wanted me to go to an emergency room with a particular symptom since he was "booked solid," and I told him, "No way, think of something else." He did: He came into the office a half-hour earlier the next morning and treated me like a valued patient of the practice, as he should have. I would have otherwise spent half a day in an emergency room with little probability of a tenth the attention but with certainty of spending ten times the duration.

You may hear some people tell you (I have, when I post these episodes on my blog) that you are self-centered, and "whining" when you complain. Allow me to complain about that rather inferior, non-Thriving attitude.

Nowhere is it written that etiquette, probity, consideration, or spirituality demands that you suffer through a bad meal; sit through a lousy performance; endure pain that could be alleviated; lose your time or money unnecessarily; or be offended by others' inappropriate behavior to your reasonable requests. Although service standards are far worse in most other parts of the world (my friends in the UK and Australia are giddy over how much better service is when they visit the U.S.), and although we are constantly besieged with why we shouldn't expect better service[75], we need to understand that nothing will change if we keep enabling others to take advantage of us.

The more we act as victims and simply bemoan our fate, the more we're correct that we are helpless.

---

[75] Airline flight attendants are *not* there primarily for our safety, which involves less than 5 percent of their time, but for our comfort, which should occupy the other 95 percent. Some just don't want to provide the service. And software manufacturers want us to believe that failures and bugs are unavoidable and we should take contingent action, rather than expect that they do it right the first time.

If you want your dreams to come true, stop allowing others to ruin them. Demand that you are treated with respect, that what you are promised is delivered, that what you were expecting is produced.

There are a variety of ways to "hit" someone. I certainly don't mean physically. But you can hit them in their pocketbook, their reputation, their ego, their brand.

Mayor Rudy Giuliani and Police Commissioner William J. Bratton reduced major crimes dramatically in New York by arresting minor violators, such as toll stile jumpers in the subway, and pick pockets on the street, and stopped treating them as a necessary evil. This led to arrests of more serious offenders and a startling improvement in public safety.

Stop winking at or merely suffering through even the minor offenses and abuses. You're simply training yourself to be a victim, to accept ever more serious abuses and shortfalls in service and support.

If you want to make it so, you can't allow others to get in the way.

Making it so

This book comes to an end in the next few pages as all books eventually do. The trick is not to let your quest to Thrive end along with it. As I always bear in mind and remind you again, George Carlin was right: "If it's someone else's book, it's not *self*-help."

So how do we "make it so" for you, and start you on the legitimate, personal journey to help yourself?

I'm a pragmatist, so here are my very practical, daily regimens to Thrive. I don't ask that you follow them all dramatically, just as I don't suggest you trod hot coals to gain confidence. But I would recommend that you view this as a menu of opportunity, and choose what will make the most sense, the most impact, and the most value for you from this day forward.

1. **Create your value inventory**. What are the "core" values that constitute your reasons for living? Are they family, friends, contributions to charity, improvement of the environment, education of yourself and others, government reform? Why are you here? What is your *raison d 'être*? What would constitute a life worth living, a legacy?

2. **Identify your daily compass heading**. What are your "operating" values? What guides you each day? Is it treating others well, providing value for others in your work and life, prospering so that you can contribute elsewhere, maintaining and building your fitness and health? What *proactively* should guide your day (as opposed to having it guided, by default, by others)?

3. **Create a time log**. Over a two-week period of "normal" work and home life (e.g., not vacations or emergencies), chart how you spend your time. Use categories for *both* time at work and not at work: phone, family recreation, meals, television, reading, assisting clients/customers, responding to superiors, social media, email, repairs, etc. Update it several times a day (you can even get time logs such as lawyers use, online or from catalogs). Determine if your actual time use matches the areas of core and operating values in your life, and whether you need to make conscious changes.

4. **Rationalize your "wishes."** Have others call you out every time you say "I wish I had....," or "wish I would have....," or "wish we didn't have to....," and so forth. Try to catch yourself, as well. Determine if these fall into categories, such as responses to peers, reactions to the boss, family situations, unexpected events, and so on. Then formulate better responses and practices using them: "I'm going to change that..." or "I can't let your comment stand without reacting to it...." or "That's just unfair and inappropriate."

5. **Identify your real fears**. Ask what you don't do, and why. Find out the real fear. If you don't offer suggestions, is it because you've been told by a loudmouth that they're "stupid"? Or do you believe there are smarter people in the room than you? Do you hesitate to eat oysters because of the texture, or to try snorkeling because you don't swim well? The more opportunities and challenges you shy away from in life, the less you Thrive. You can tell me you don't like uni (sea urchin, a Japanese delicacy) because you've tasted it and it's unpleasant for you, but not by just looking at it. (If you didn't know what uni is, then you're already in too limited a life.)

6. **Become an opportunist, not a "list maker."** The most boring people I know have "life lists" of 50 or 500 things to accomplish, many rather daunting (climb Mt. Everest), many *de rigeuer* (see Machu Picchu), and many idiosyncratic (set the pogo stick record). It's far better to be opportunistic. Thriving is about being in the moment, not a slave to guidelines set when you were a different person with different needs. You're far better off jumping on a plane to spend an impulsive weekend in Nantucket than you are saving that money for your eventual excursion to Antarctica in five more years. Live for the moment and in the moment. (You can still go to Antarctica, perhaps impulsively, some day. Maybe on a pogo stick.)

7. **Stop taking "no" for a reply, response, resolution, or reaction**. If something is important, find a way to get it done. A sense of healthy outrage and a determination to rectify a wrong is quite different from whining as a victim. What are you being prevented from doing that is important because of someone's "no"? If the cable company, or the town public works director, or an airline customer service clerk, or a hotel concierge is not providing the answers you need, go over their heads. A traffic cop has a right to stop you from speeding, because it endangers

public welfare. A hotel clerk does not have the right to tell you that you can't have a late checkout, because the hotel does it every day for innumerable people.

8. **Don your own oxygen mask**. Are you fit? Are you happy about your health? Do you have the wardrobe that you need for success in your profession and comfort in your personal life? Are you driving a safe and efficient car for your purposes? Do you have the tools, the resources, the time you need to be successful and supportive? If not, get them. Exhibit a healthy selfishness. If you want to bestow time, attention, gifts, resources, even wealth, on others, then you must have enough to sustain yourself and provide for others. *Subsistence farming is one thing, subsistence living is another. You need to produce excess in order to distribute it. And that includes happiness.*

9. **Inventory your assets**. We grow based on strengths and exploiting what we're good at and passionate about. What assets do you have that are not employed, or not exploited? Are you spending more time trying to "fix" weaknesses than advance strengths? The first step is to assess what your behavioral, experiential, competency, educational, credential, and other strengths are. Then make a plan to use them frequently and well, and you'll see your life change.

10. **Make it so**. Create a priority list for tomorrow based on these conditions and the notes and impact you've gained from this book. It should be a maximum of three items, and mere "chunks" of large issues are fine. If you want to write a book, then write a book proposal or a chapter over the next week, for example. If you want to run for president of your club or professional association, then start by talking to a few key potential supporters. You get the idea. Just three important "chunks" a day, every day, personal or professional, but achievable. Actually, that's the way they climb Mt. Everest, in stages.

Don't say "I wish I had read this book when I was younger"! Don't worry about perfect adherence to its principles and advice, but focus on your personal success. There is no perfect moment to begin Thriving. But there is a great time to move from trying to survive to trying to Thrive.

And that time is now. I asked at the conclusion of the introduction if you're ready to embark on a great personal and career journey. If you're not ready now, you'll never be.

Make it so.

Books to Thrive

Notes on these selections: I've chosen to include only a single work of any author. Otherwise, I'd list every book that John Updike, Patrick O'Brian, Stephan Jay Gould and others ever wrote. I've omitted business books, since I think most are boring and you learn far more about business from fiction and historical works. As any such list, this one is idiosyncratic, but I've read every word on every page in every book, and you would be able to chat with virtually anyone about anything if you consumed them all. Alas, I've had to omit foreign language books that have not been translated, though I read *L'Etranger* by Jean-Paul Sartre in the original French, and I've never quite recovered. Many of the historical novels are chosen as much for their education in history, geography, and economies as they are for their story lines.

I've included humor, athletics, science fiction, warfare, biography, philosophy, science, horror, and just great stories. I'm not annotating them so that you have to work a bit. But I'll tell you this: Patrick O'Brian's series on the British Navy is the best of its genre, ever. *The Grapes of Wrath* and *The Great Gatsby* may be the two best novels ever written by Americans, as is *Madame Bovary* by a Frenchman. *The Rising Sun*, a Pulitzer Prize winner for John Toland, is the best explanation of the war in the Pacific you will ever read.

Of course, you couldn't go wrong going through all of Shakespeare's plays, either.

Fiction

A Tale of Two Cities: Charles Dickens

Advise and Consent: Allen Drury

An American Dream: Norman Mailer

An American Tragedy: Theodore Dreiser

Anna Karenina: Leo Tolstoy

Atlas Shrugged: Ayn Rand

Candide: Voltaire

Catch 22: Joseph Heller

Crime and Punishment: Fyodor Dostoevsky

Cujo: Stephen King

Deliverance: James Dickey

Ethan Frome: Edith Wharton

Foundation: Isaac Asimov

Hamlet: Shakespeare

Hotel New Hampshire: John Irving

Invisible Man: Ralph Ellison

Jaws: Peter Benchley

Jude the Obscure: Thomas Hardy

Madame Bovary: Gustave Flaubert

Main Street: Sinclair Lewis

Master and Commander: Patrick O'Brian

Maximum Bob: Elmore Leonard

Moby Dick: Herman Melville

Pride and Prejudice: Jane Austen

Rabbit Run: John Updike

Roots: Alex Haley

Semi-Tough: Dan Jenkins

Shogun: James Clavell

Stranger in A Strange Land: Robert Heinlein

The Agony and the Ecstasy: Irving Stone

The American: Henry James

The Andromeda Strain: Michael Crichton

The Devil's Advocate: Morris West

The Godfather: Mario Puzo

The Grapes of Wrath: John Steinbeck
The Great Gatsby: F. Scott Fitzgerald
The Hunt for Red October: Tom Clancy
The Iliad: Homer
The Jungle: Upton Sinclair
The Last Angry Man: Gerald Green
The Prince of Tides: Pat Conroy
The Winds of War: Herman Wouk
The Year the Yankees Lost the Pennant: Douglass Wallop

Non-Fiction

A Distant Mirror: Barbara Tuchman
A Stillness At Appomattox: Bruce Catton
All Creatures Great and Small: James Herriot
Black Night, White Snow: Harrison Salisbury
Boca's Brain: Carl Sagan
Einstein: Walter Isaacson
1491: Charles Mann
Freedom At Midnight: Larry Collins and Dominique Lapierre
From Dawn to Decadence: Jacques Barzun
Hard Times: Studs Turkel
In God We Trust: Jean Shepherd
John Adams: David McCullough
John Paul Jones: Evan Thomas
Leviathan: Thomas Hobbes
Team of Rivals: Doris Kearns Goodwin
The Arms of Krupp: William Manchester
The Boys of Summer: Roger Kahn
The Human Condition: Hannah Arendt
The Lunatic Express: Charles Miller
The Medium Is the Message: Marshall McLuhan
The Mismeasure of Man: Stephen Jay Gould
The Right Stuff: Tom Wolfe
The Rising Sun: John Toland
The World Is Flat: Thomas Friedman

About the Author

Alan Weiss is one of those rare people who can say he is a consultant, speaker and author and mean it. His consulting firm, Summit Consulting Group, Inc. has attracted clients such as Merck, Hewlett-Packard, GE, Mercedes-Benz, State Street Corporation, Times Mirror Group, The Federal Reserve, Toyota, The New York Times Corporation, and over 500 other leading organizations. He has served on the boards of directors of the Trinity Repertory Company, a Tony-Award-winning New England regional theater, Festival Ballet Providence, Gamm Theater, and has chaired the Newport International Film Festival.

His speaking typically includes 30 keynotes a year at major conferences, and he has been a visiting faculty member at Case Western Reserve University, Boston College, Tufts, St. John's, the University of Illinois, the Institute of Management Studies, and the University of Georgia Graduate School of Business. He has held an appointment as adjunct professor in the Graduate School of Business at the University of Rhode Island where he taught courses on advanced management and consulting skills. He has held the record for selling out the highest priced workshop (on entrepreneurialism) in the history of New York City's Learning Annex. His Ph.D. is in psychology and he is a member of the American Psychological Society, the American Counseling Association, Division 13 of the American Psychological Association, and the Society for Personality and Social Psychology.

He has served on the Board of Governors of Harvard University's Center for Mental Health and the Media. He has keynoted for the American Psychological Association on two occasions.

He is an inductee into the Professional Speaking Hall of Fame® and the concurrent recipient of the National Speakers Association Council of Peers Award of Excellence (CPAE), representing the top 1% of professional speakers in the world. He has been named a Fellow of the Institute of Management Consultants (FCMC), one of only two people in history holding both those designations.

His prolific publishing includes over 1,000 articles and 35 books, including his bestseller, *Million Dollar Consulting* (from McGraw-Hill). His newest prior to this one is *The Talent Advantage* (with Dr. Nancy MacKay, John Wiley and Sons, 2009). His books have been on the curricula at Villanova, Temple University, and the Wharton School of Business, and have been translated into German, Italian, Arabic, Spanish, Russian, Korean, and Chinese.

He is interviewed and quoted frequently in the media. His career has taken him to 58 countries and 49 states. (He is afraid to go to North Dakota.) *Success Magazine* has cited him in an editorial devoted to his work as "a worldwide expert in executive education." *The New York Post* calls him "one of the most highly regarded independent consultants in America." He is the winner of the prestigious Axiem Award for Excellence in Audio Presentation.

In 2006 he was presented with the Lifetime Achievement Award of the American Press Institute, the first-ever for a non-journalist, and one of only seven awarded in the 60-year history of the association.

He has coached the former and present Miss Rhode Island/Miss America candidates in interviewing skills. He once appeared on the popular American TV game show *Jeopardy*, where he lost badly in the first round to a dancing waiter from Iowa.

Index